THE UNOFFICIAL HARRY POTTER COMPLETE PUZZLE BOOK

Ultimate Fan Trivia Presented by MuggleNet

Reveal the secrets of Hogwarts with brainteasers, puzzles, riddles and more!

Topix Media Lab
For inquiries, call 646-449-8614

Published by Topix Media Lab
14 Wall Street, Suite 3C
New York, NY 10005

Printed in China

ISBN-13: 978-1-956403-18-3
ISBN-10: 1-956403-18-3

CEO Tony Romando

Vice President & Publisher Phil Sexton
Senior Vice President of Sales & New Markets Tom Mifsud
Vice President of Retail Sales & Logistics Linda Greenblatt
Chief Financial Officer Vandana Patel
Manufacturing Director Nancy Puskuldjian
Financial Analyst Matthew Quinn
Digital Marketing & Strategy Manager Elyse Gregov

Chief Content Officer Jeff Ashworth
Director of Editorial Operations Courtney Kerrigan
Creative Director Susan Dazzo
Photo Director Dave Weiss

Issue Editor Tim Baker
Issue Designer Glen Karpowich
Senior Editor Trevor Courneen
Associate Editor Juliana Sharaf
Assistant Managing Editor Tara Sherman
Designer Mikio Sakai
Copy Editor & Fact Checker Madeline Raynor
Junior Designer Alyssa Bredin Quirós
Assistant Photo Editor Jenna Addesso

MuggleNet
The #1 Wizarding World Resource Since 1999

Creative & Marketing Director Kat Miller
Managing Editor Felicia Grady

Special thanks to MuggleNet staff for the following features:

"Did You Know?" trivia (throughout) Aly Kirk, Amanda Halmes, Carolyn Sehgal, Marica Laing, Richa Venkatraman and Victoria Durgin

O.W.L. Exams (pg. 146-155)
Marica Laing, Marissa Osman, Rex Hadden, Richa Venkatraman and Victoria Durgin

The Half-Blood Prince's Textbook (pg. 196-197)
Carolyn Sehgal, Jennifer Creevy, John L. Wilda, Kimira V. Leonard and Sas Rhodes

N.E.W.T. Exams (pg. 206-213)
Elizabeth Pease, Marissa Osman, Rex Hadden and Richa Venkatraman

Fact-checking by Catherine Lai

TM22-04

A Wizarding Test

FOR MORE THAN two decades, the wondrous wizarding world of *Harry Potter* has inspired imaginations around the world, building a fan base larger than perhaps any other fictional property. In the following pages, the experts at MuggleNet offer the ultimate challenge for millions of loyal readers: *The Unofficial Harry Potter Complete Puzzle Book*. Packed with unique ways for you to test your wizarding world knowledge, it's sure to keep you occupied whether you're killing time aboard the Hogwarts Express or taking a break from studying for your O.W.L.s. Test your knowledge of the entire *Harry Potter* saga with expert-level trivia, mazes, wizarding games, codebreaking and much, much more!

COVER AND BACK COVER: SHUTTERSTOCK

Harry Potter and the Sorcerer's Stone

How well do you know the ins and outs of our first look at the wizarding world?

WARNER BROS/MOVIESTILLSDB

Did You Know?

This book opens on November 1, 1981, the day after James and Lily Potter were murdered by Lord Voldemort.

First-years approach Hogwarts by boat in *Harry Potter and the Sorcerer's Stone* (2001).

Fill-In-The Blanks

During his first year at __________ School of __________ and ____________, Harry Potter learns he is the most famous wizard alive—known, thanks to his defeat of Dark wizard ___________ as an infant, as The ___ Who __________. Whisked away from his home at 4 __________ ________, Harry is introduced to the wizarding world by a bevy of new friends including __________ Hagrid, Ron __________ and ____________ Granger, and above all, Headmaster _________ ____________. The latter wizard begins the long task of preparing Harry for his ultimate battle with _____________. He learns to play __________ thanks to _________, the stern but fair head of ____________ House, and even manages to put a _____ -_____ _____ named _____ to sleep by playing __________. Little does anyone know, however, that He _____ ____ _____ _____ _______ lurks nearby under the guise of Defense Against the Dark Arts Professor _________.

Daniel Radcliffe as Harry Potter, Rupert Grint as Ron Weasley and Emma Watson as Hermione Granger in *Harry Potter and the Sorcerer's Stone* (2001).

Find Your Wizarding Wares

Based on your knowledge of the wizarding world, can you fill in the names of the missing Diagon Alley businesses on the map below?

A tavern that features the entrance to Diagon Alley in its yard.

1

2

This alliterative business sells frozen treats.

A wand chooses a wizard here.

3

4

Where Harry first sets his eyes on a Nimbus 2000.

CLOCKWISE FROM TOP LEFT: WARNER BROS/MOVIESTILLSDB; SHUTTERSTOCK (2); UNITED ARCHIVES GMBH/ALAMY; WARNER BROS/MOVIESTILLSDB; SHUTTERSTOCK (2)

Clockwise from top left: Daniel Radcliffe as Harry Potter and John Hurt as Ollivander in *Harry Potter and the Sorcerer's Stone* (2001); Slytherin robe costumes on display; Gringotts goblins in *Harry Potter and the Sorcerer's Stone* (2001); Daniel Radcliffe as Harry Potter and Kenneth Branagh as Gilderoy Lockhart in *Harry Potter and the Chamber of Secrets* (2002).

Harry first meets Draco Malfoy in this clothing store.

6

Hagrid buys Harry's birthday present in *Sorcerer's Stone* at this store.

7

8

Depository of wizarding wealth.

5

Where Harry picks up *The Standard Book of Spells.*

Did You Know?

Only four spells appear in this book: *Alohomora*, *Locomotor Mortis*, *Petrificus Totalus* and *Wingardium Leviosa*.

Sorcerer's Stone

Warwick Davis as the Gringotts teller in *Harry Potter and the Sorcerer's Stone* (2001).

WARNER BROS/EVERETT COLLECTION

A Robbery At Gringotts

Thieves have broken into the Diagon Alley institution and made off with treasures of immense value. Can you help the bank's goblin employees figure out what else has been stolen?

INVENTORY LIST

The total amount stolen was valued at *144,000 Galleons.* Of the 12 items stolen, seven of them have already been figured to be worth a total of *72,000 Galleons.*

12,750 Galleons	Antique Foe-Glass
4,990 Galleons	Goblin-Made Dagger
16,840 Galleons	Jeweled Pensieve
19,000 Galleons	Gold Ingots
26,850 Galleons	Signed First Edition, *Quidditch Through the Ages*
8,050 Galleons	Original Pressing, Merlin Chocolate Frog Card
14,360 Galleons	Solid Gold Omnioculars
20,000 Galleons	Uncut Sapphires, Rubies and Opals

Can you use addition, subtraction and the vault's remaining inventory (provided) to determine which five additional items were taken?

____

____

Hogwarts Class of '98

The Hogwarts great hall seen in the *Harry Potter* films, pictured, is modeled after the Great Hall at Christ Church in Oxford, England.

FROM LEFT: RGR COLLECTION/ALAMY; WARNER BROS/MOVIESTILLSDB

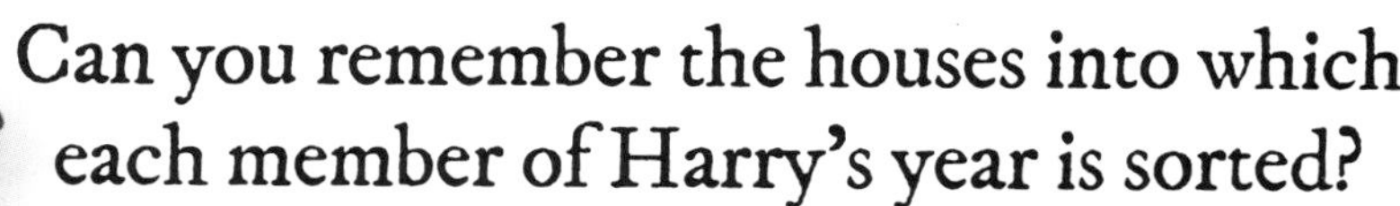

Can you remember the houses into which each member of Harry's year is sorted?

Name	House
Daphne Greengrass	
Seamus Finnigan	G
Parvati Patil	
Draco Malfoy	S
Vincent Crabbe	S
Ernie Macmillan	
Justin Finch-Fletchley	
Wayne Hopkins	
Hannah Abbott	
Susan Bones	H
Anthony Goldstein	
Lavender Brown	R
Michael Corner	
Terry Boot	
Dean Thomas	G
Padma Patil	G
Mandy Brocklehurst	
Lisa Turpin	
Hermione Granger	G
Harry Potter	G
Gregory Goyle	S
Theodore Nott	
Neville Longbottom	G
Blaise Zabini	
Pansy Parkinson	
Ron Weasley	G
Millicent Bulstrode	H

Gryffindor

Hufflepuff

Ravenclaw

Slytherin

First-Year Curriculum

Can you find the words and phrases that proved important for Harry Potter's first-year studies at Hogwarts?

This creature, also a failing O.W.L. and N.E.W.T. grade, causes a panic at Halloween.

____

This spell is used by Hermione in the film to fix Harry's glasses on the Hogwarts Express.

____

Hermione and Ron plan to use this "leg-locker" curse on Professor Snape if he attempts to harm Harry during a Quidditch match.

____

Hermione chides Ron for not being able to properly pronounce this levitation spell.

____

This stone, found in a goat's stomach, is used in potions.

____

This potion ingredient is also known as monkshood and aconite.

____

Making his way through the Forbidden Forest with Hagrid, Harry meets members of this horse hybrid species.

____

Hagrid's trusty canine companion, Fang, is described in the books as what breed?

____

Professor Quirrell, supposedly afraid of attack from vampires, wears a necklace of this fragrant flower used in cooking.

____

M G Y E U P S R H B M L T R O L L
Y Q A C F Q X Y E C J V D J P D O
D A W H P E D B W B M Y B L A J R
Q K H F N O B L J W E M Z C U Z A
W C Z M U D D J R U D I H M F O Y
W R L V Y U W I S A E B I F H P A
T I J T L C L L K V X W G X Q G U
G S N L P D F O Z C E N T A U R U
L Y B G V J B L Y A Q P G F V S K
O M O T A R N X N O B O G G A A C
C S J D K R H W S I L C S K H C S
O B H M R J D X J W U U D P U E M
M H G P J W K I Z X Y L D Q Y Z R
O E A M Z O Q K U P B U C Q I A T
T Y R N B L X I Z M Q S B A H H J
O X L F O F V S I Y L R K G Y H I
R Q I B A S I G I F B E L W S M S
M Y C E R B D E Q H U P V F A L C
O F H Z H A A L N W W A W I F I A
R I H O O N A H B B J R U V O U M
T J D A U E S H J A A O X U R S D
I Z K R N Z R P A Q I H D Q T N A
S W N L D A Y B E P R K G M R J N

Hogwarts Curriculum: Year 1

How closely were you paying attention to the *Harry Potter* books and films?

1. Scenes in the Hogwarts library's restricted section were filmed at which historic U.K. university?
A. Cambridge
B. The London School of Economics
C. Oxford
D. St. Andrews

2. What does the inscription above the Mirror of Erised say? ______________

3. Three "actors," named Gizmo, Ook and Sprout, shared which role in *Harry Potter and the Sorcerer's Stone*?
A. Hedwig
B. Scabbers
C. Mrs. Norris
D. Errol

4. Beginning with *Sorcerer's Stone*, Daniel Radcliffe went through 160 of these while filming the series.
A. Wands
B. Robes
C. Broomsticks
D. Pairs of Glasses

5. Astute viewers might notice a trophy "for services to Hogwarts" won by this student next to a Quidditch award during Harry's detention scene.

____

6. This part, played by Rik Mayall, was cut from the film and never revisited in the series.

____

7. What kind of sandwiches does Mrs. Weasley pack for Ron's journey to Hogwarts, forgetting he doesn't like them?

____

8. Where does the first act of Transfiguration we see performed by Professor McGonagall in the film take place?

____

9. Ron uses *Wingardium Leviosa* successfully for the first time on which holiday evening?

____

10. What is the first treat Harry tastes off the Hogwarts Express trolley?

____

11. In the book, which character gave Harry each of his Christmas presents during his first year?
A. A 50-pence piece ______________
B. Homemade fudge and a sweater ______________
C. Chocolate Frogs ______________
D. Wooden flute ______________
E. Invisibility cloak ______________

Daniel Radcliffe as
Harry Potter.

Hogwarts Curriculum: Year 1

How closely were you paying attention to the *Harry Potter* books and films?

Maggie Smith as Minerva McGonagall in *Harry Potter and the Sorcerer's Stone* (2001).

12. Though it's cast nonverbally, the first spell Harry sees in *Harry Potter and the Sorcerer's Stone* is a Transfiguration spell that changes the appearance of which character?

____

13. The Gryffindor first years watch Professor McGonagall turn her desk into a _____ during their first Transfiguration lesson.

14. Ron, first unable to master the incantation, uses this levitation spell to save Hermione from a giant troll. ______________________________

15. This spell used by Hermione to get into the third floor corridor is also known as the "Thief's Friend." _________________________

16. Neville is the first *Harry Potter* character to be hit with a full body bind, signified by which incantation?

____

Can you match the chapter name to what happened within it?

Chapter Name	What Occurred
1. The Boy Who Lived __	**A.** Harry becomes a member of Gryffindor House.
2. Diagon Alley __	**B.** Harry Potter is dropped off on his aunt and uncle's doorstep.
3. The Sorting Hat __	**C.** During detention with Hagrid, Harry encounters Voldemort.
4. The Mirror of Erised __	**D.** Harry is introduced to the wizarding world.
5. The Forbidden Forest __	**E.** Harry stops Quirrell from stealing the Sorcerer's Stone.
6. The Man With Two Faces __	**F.** Harry sees his deepest heart's desire.

The Hogwarts "Alma Mater"

FILL IN THE BLANKS

Hogwarts, Hogwarts, ____
____ Hogwarts,
____ us something please,
Whether we be old and ___
Or young with _____ knees,
Our ____ could do with filling
With some _______ stuff,
For now they're bare and full of
___, Dead ____ and bits of fluff,
So teach us things worth ______,
Bring back what we've forgot,
Just do your best, we'll do the rest,
And learn until our brains
all ___.

Members of the Hogwarts Frog Choir, conducted by Professor Flitwick, practice their harmonies.

Be the Sorting Hat

Based on their attributes, can you Sort the following students into the correct Hogwarts House?

Name William B. Snidely
Residence Mayfair, London, England
Favorite School Subject Herbology, as both his Muggle parents are florists and it feels familiar.
Biggest Ambition for Hogwarts To help his friends earn the House Cup.
Ideal Vacation Tapas Tour of Spain
Friends Describe Him As Affable, Understanding, Capable

____

Name Shep Holbrook
Residence Cardiff, Wales
Favorite School Subject Potions—anyone can be a master potion-maker if they follow the directions to a T.
Biggest Ambition at Hogwarts To earn the highest possible marks on all of his N.E.W.T.s, setting himself up for a stellar career.
Ideal Vacation A week-long pass to the restricted section of the Hogwarts Library.
Friends Describe Him As Sardonic, Bookish, Easily Bored

____

Name Gwinnifer Gaines
Residence Gaines Manor, Fife, Scotland
Favorite School Subject History of Magic—the pageant of noble pureblood wizards of old makes her yearn for a better, simpler time.
Biggest Ambition at Hogwarts To attach her name to as many accomplishments and records as possible so no one will forget her name.
Ideal Vacation Semester-long exchange program with Durmstrang.
Friends Describe Her As Calculating, Isolated, Focused

Name Edwina Runkle
Residence Ottery St. Catchpole, England
Favorite School Subject Defense Against the Dark Arts—She's wanted to be in Magical Law Enforcement since her Auror aunt was killed in the Wizarding Wars.
Biggest Ambition for Hogwarts To become Head Girl.
Ideal Vacation Time off? She'd rather shadow someone at the Ministry of Magic to earn valuable experience.
Friends Describe Her As Loyal, Intelligent, Fearless

Daniel Radcliffe as Harry Potter and Tom Felton as Draco Malfoy in *Harry Potter and the Sorcerer's Stone* (2001).

TCD/PROD.DB/ALAMY

The Forbidden Forest

Harry is serving detention in the Forbidden Forest with Draco Malfoy and Fang. Can you lead them out of the woods?

Sorcerer's Stone

Wandlore Wisdom

As a first-year, Harry meets Ollivander, a man who never forgets a face or wand. Can you remember which wand belongs to whom?

________________ 1. 11" holly, phoenix feather, nice and supple. Known for its use of disarming spells.

________________ 2. 10", hawthorn, unicorn hair, reasonably springy. Changes owners in Book Seven.

________________ 3. 12", ash, unicorn hair. Splits in Book Two.

________________ 4. 13½", yew, phoenix feather—Fawkes's feather, to be precise.

________________ 5. 12¾", walnut, dragon heartstring, unyielding. Loses a duel to Molly Weasley.

________________ 6. 10¾", vine, dragon heartstring. Used for ocular repair in the first film.

________________ 7. 14", willow, unicorn hair. Used to stop a rain storm in a Ministry of Magic office.

________________ 8. 8", birch, dragon heartstring. Nearly performs an unforgivable curse on a Hogwarts student.

Daniel Radcliffe as Harry Potter in *Harry Potter and the Sorcerer's Stone* (2001).

Sorcerer's Stone

Magic Shadows

Can you tell which of the silhouettes opposite is a direct match?

COLLECTION CHRISTOPHEL/ALAMY

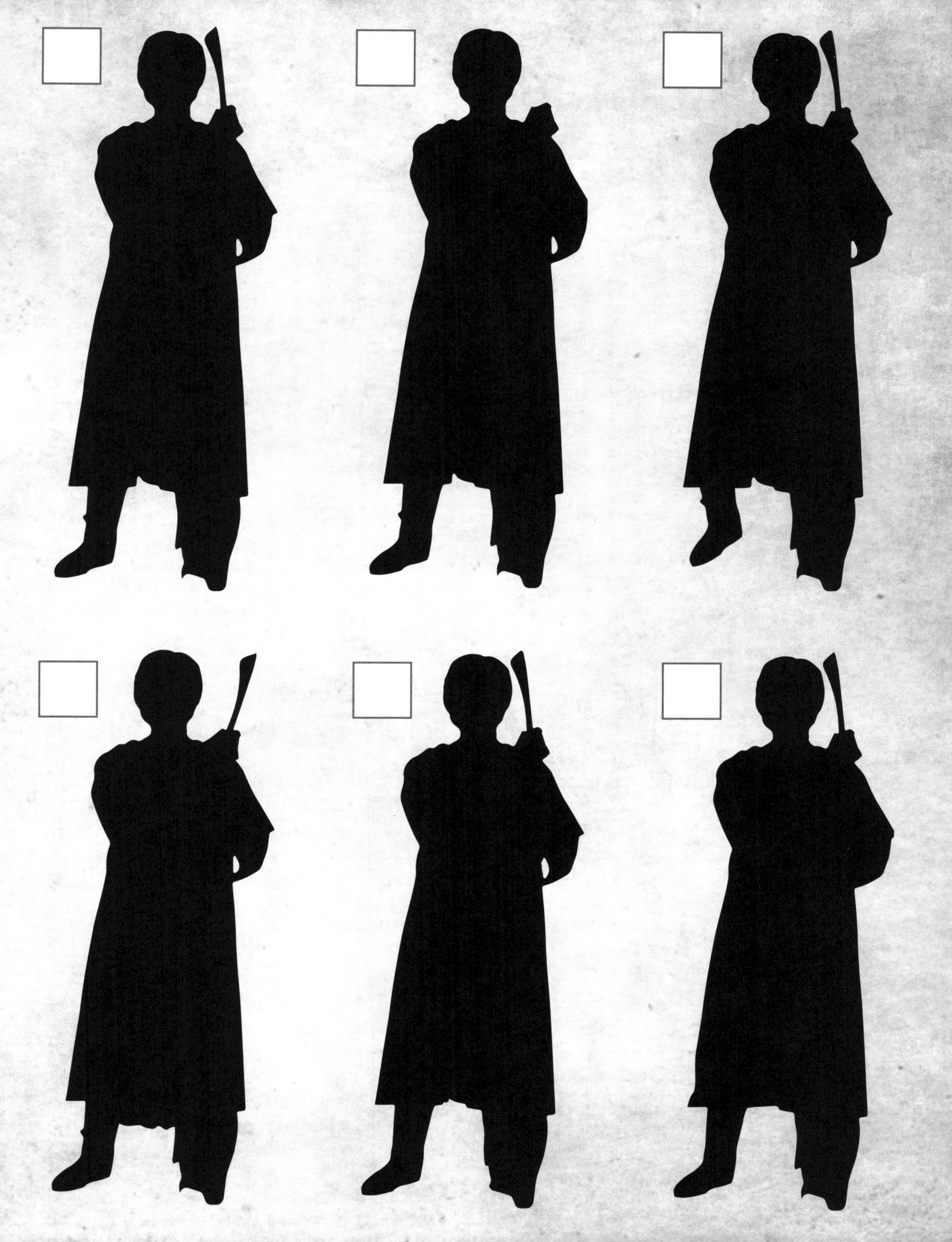

Teacher of the Year

1. Harry first meets Professor Quirrell in this wizarding locale:

____

2. Professor Quirrell's classroom is described as smelling like this plant:

____

3. Quirrell claims to have gotten his turban from a prince for ridding his kingdom of which magical creature?
A. Sphinx

B. Boggart

C. Grindylow

D. Zombie

4. What is Professor Quirrell's first name?
A. Quintus

B. Quentin

C. Quirinus

D. Quarl

5. In the movie, Professor Quirrell is holding an iguana when Professor McGonagall comes to his classroom to inquire about which student?

____

Professor Quirrell

Ian Hart as Professor Quirrell in *Harry Potter and the Sorcerer's Stone* (2001).

Emma Watson as Hermione Granger, Rupert Grint as Ron Weasley and Daniel Radcliffe as Harry Potter in *Harry Potter and the Sorcerer's Stone* (2001).

Checkmate Challenge

Can you end these games in one move and prove you're ready to play Gryffindor's best?

GRYFFINDOR'S RESIDENT chess master is tired of beating everyone all the time, so they've created some brain-building puzzles to help other members of the House hone their skills. Hopefully, after solving all of these, you'll be able to give the chess expert and their trusty old wizard chess set a decent challenge. Playing as white, can you reach checkmate in one move on each of the following boards?

1. ______________

2. ______________

1
2
3
4
5
6
7
8
A B C D E F G H

3. ______________________

4. ______________________

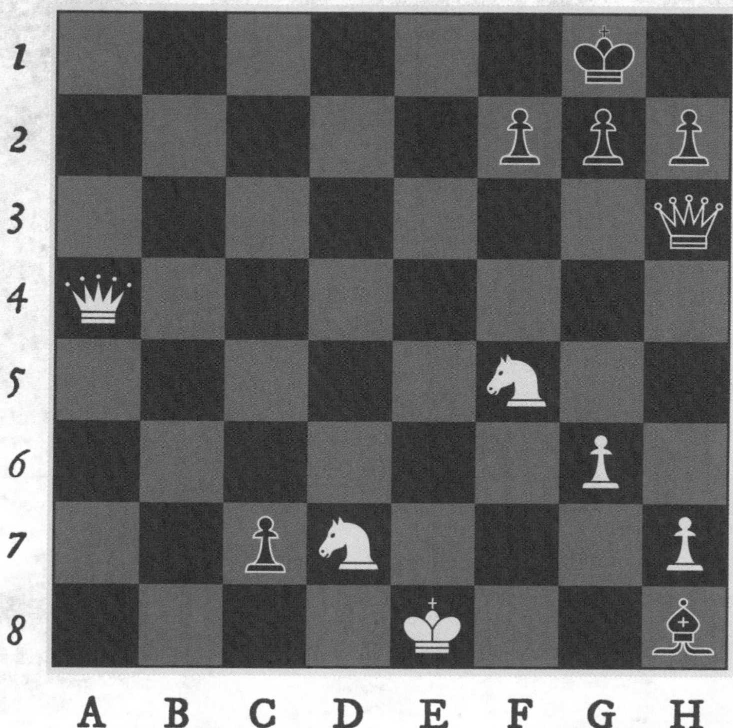

5. ______________

6. ______________

MuggleNet's Expert Trivia: Year 1

You must have been paying close attention to every word of the saga if you can answer all of these questions.

1. Who was the first caretaker of Hogwarts?

____

2. Which Hogwarts professor was named after their grandmother?

____

3. Which Hogwarts professor directed Hogwarts's one and only Christmas play?

____

4. Which broom did Madam Hooch learn to fly on?

____

COLLECTION CHRISTOPHEL/ALAMY

Zoë Wanamaker as Madam Hooch teaches first-year students how to fly in *Harry Potter and the Sorcerer's Stone* (2001).

Harry Potter and the Chamber of Secrets

The Heir of Slytherin is loose once again at Hogwarts. And Harry, as usual, is caught in the middle.

PICTURELUX/THE HOLLYWOOD ARCHIVE/ALAMY

Did You Know?

Tom Marvolo Riddle's name changes slightly throughout translations of the *Harry Potter* books to accommodate the "I am Lord Voldemort" anagram he spells in the Chamber of Secrets. In French, for example, his name is Tom Elvis Jedusor.

The flying Ford Anglia and the Hogwarts Express in *Harry Potter and the Chamber of Secrets* (2002).

Fill-In-The Blanks

After defeating Voldemort with the help of The _______ of ________, which showed him with the ________ ________ in his pocket, Harry returns to Hogwarts for his second year. After being delayed by a house-elf named _______, he is rescued by ____, _______ and ____ Weasley in their _______'s flying Ford ________, soon to be destroyed by the _________ __________. Once the second year gets underway, strange things begin happening at Hogwarts, attributed to a mysterious figure known as the _____ of __________. This villain claims to have opened the _______ of _______, from which a deadly _________ escapes, Petrifying Muggle-born students. Because he was expelled from Hogwarts the last time such a series of events occurred, ________ is sent to _________. But Harry and his friends are willing to do anything to save Hogwarts. With the help of a _______ named ________ ________, they find the entrance to the chamber and face off against Tom Riddle, reanimated thanks to his magically-altered _______. Before their battle, Riddle reveals himself to be none other than _________, but with the help of ________ the _______, Harry is triumphant yet again.

PICTURELUX/THE HOLLYWOOD ARCHIVE/ALAMY

Rupert Grint as Ron Weasley, Daniel Radcliffe as Harry Potter and Emma Watson as Hermione Granger.

New Friends, New Foes

Can you unscramble the names of the characters introduced in the second installment of Harry Potter's Hogwarts saga?

RGAAOG

____

BOBYD

____

RAUHTR ALWSEYE

____

TMO ERDIDL

____

LCONI EECVERY

____

CULISU LAFYOM

____

RM. OBGRNI

NMAINOG YLRTME

IGLEODRY LCOHRAKT

Did You Know?

While Harry helps Lockhart sign fan mail, he tells Harry about Gladys Gudgeon, a "huge fan of mine." In *Order of the Phoenix*, Lockhart is in St. Mungo's with his memory modified and can't figure out why Gladys Gudgeon writes to him weekly.

Toby Jones provided the voice for Dobby in *Harry Potter and the Chamber of Secrets* (2002).

FOR BONUS HOUSE POINTS

Arthur Weasley's Silly Circuits

Mr. Weasley, whom Harry meets in *Chamber of Secrets*, is notoriously fascinated with Muggle technology and has decided to start learning about electricity. Can you help him locate the correct piece to fill in his panel without causing a short circuit?

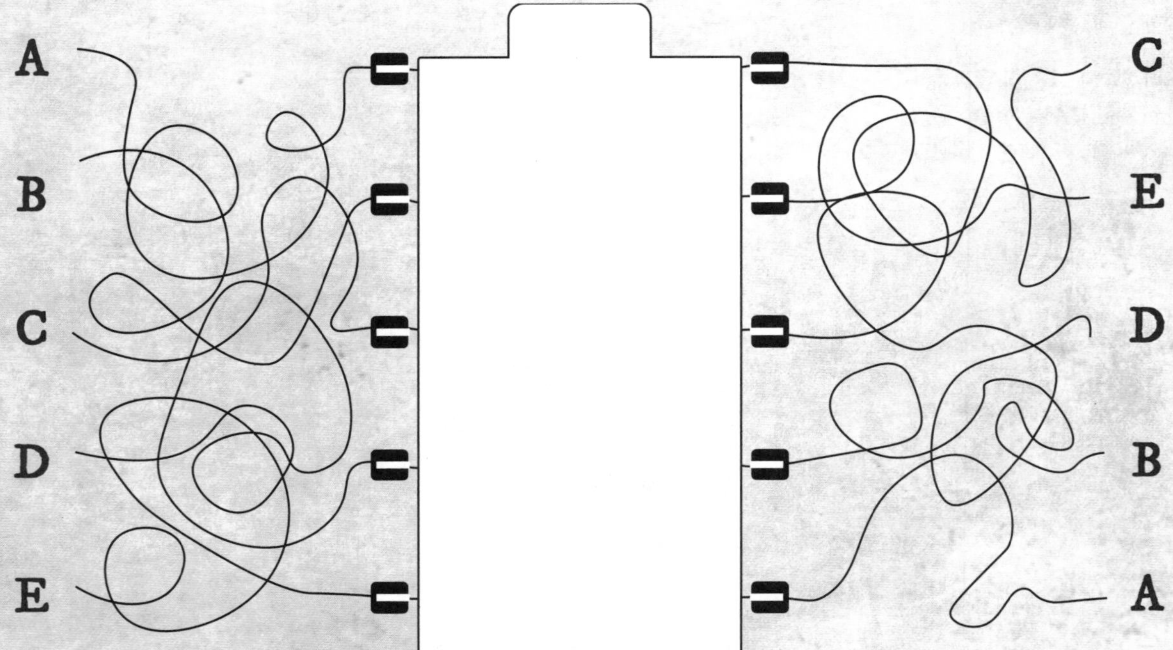

Puzzle Tip

One of the wire schemes provided will line up perfectly with the wires in Mr. Weasley's circuit board. The others will cause a shocking short circuit and ruin his experiment.

WARNER BROS/EVERETT COLLECTION

The Weasleys visit their oldest son Bill in Egypt, where he is working for Gringotts.

Arthur Weasley's Silly Circuits

Mr. Weasley is notoriously fascinated with Muggle technology and has decided to start learning about electricity. Can you help him locate the correct piece to fill in his panel without causing a short circuit?

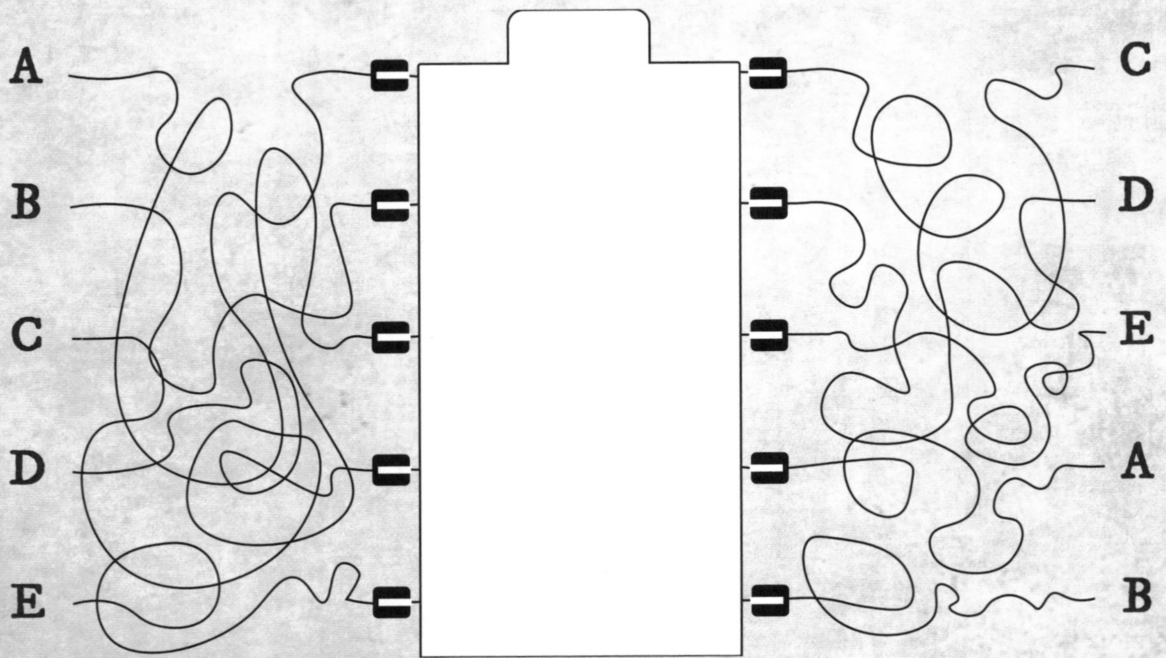

Puzzle Tip

One of the wire schemes provided will line up perfectly with the wires in Mr. Weasley's circuit board. The others will cause a shocking short circuit and ruin his experiment.

Mark Willams as
Arthur Weasley.

FOR BONUS HOUSE POINTS

Arthur Weasley's Silly Circuits

Mr. Weasley is notoriously fascinated with Muggle technology and has decided to start learning about electricity. Can you help him locate the correct piece to fill in his panel without causing a short circuit?

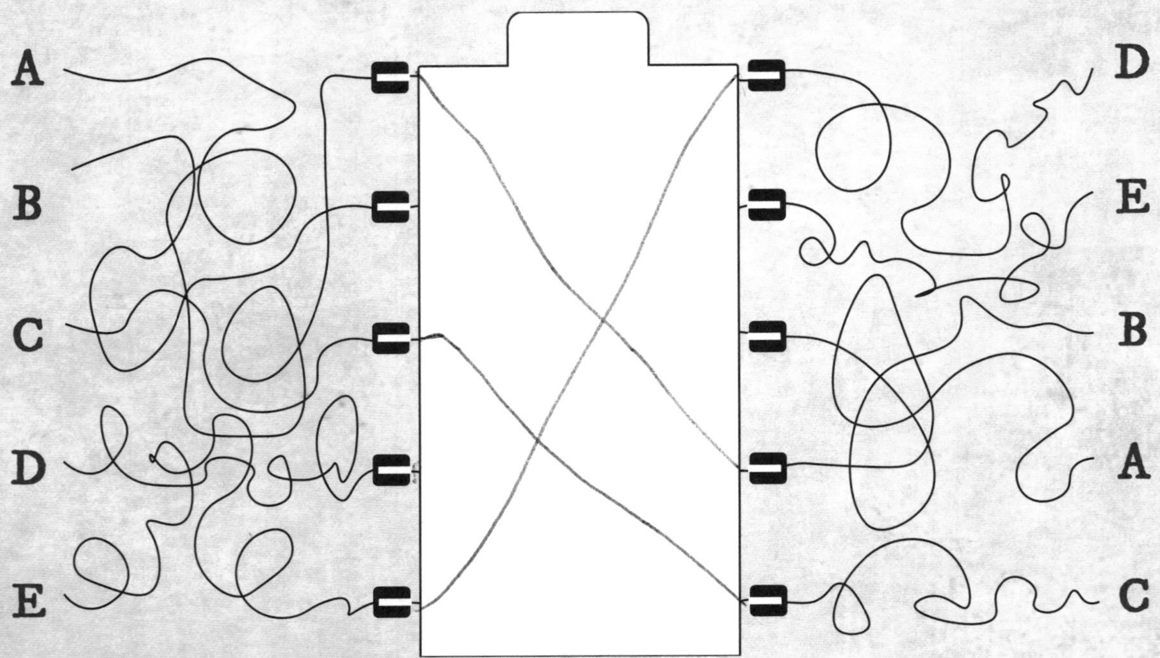

Puzzle Tip

One of the wire schemes provided will line up perfectly with the wires in Mr. Weasley's circuit board. The others will cause a shocking short circuit and ruin his experiment.

WARNER BROS/EVERETT COLLECTION

Mr. Weasley leads the way to the Quidditch World Cup in *Harry Potter and the Goblet of Fire* (2005).

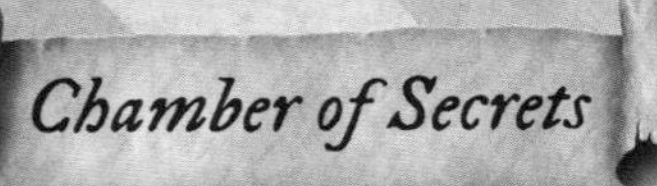

Magic Shadows

Can you tell which of the silhouettes opposite is a direct match?

WARNER BROS/EVERETT COLLECTION

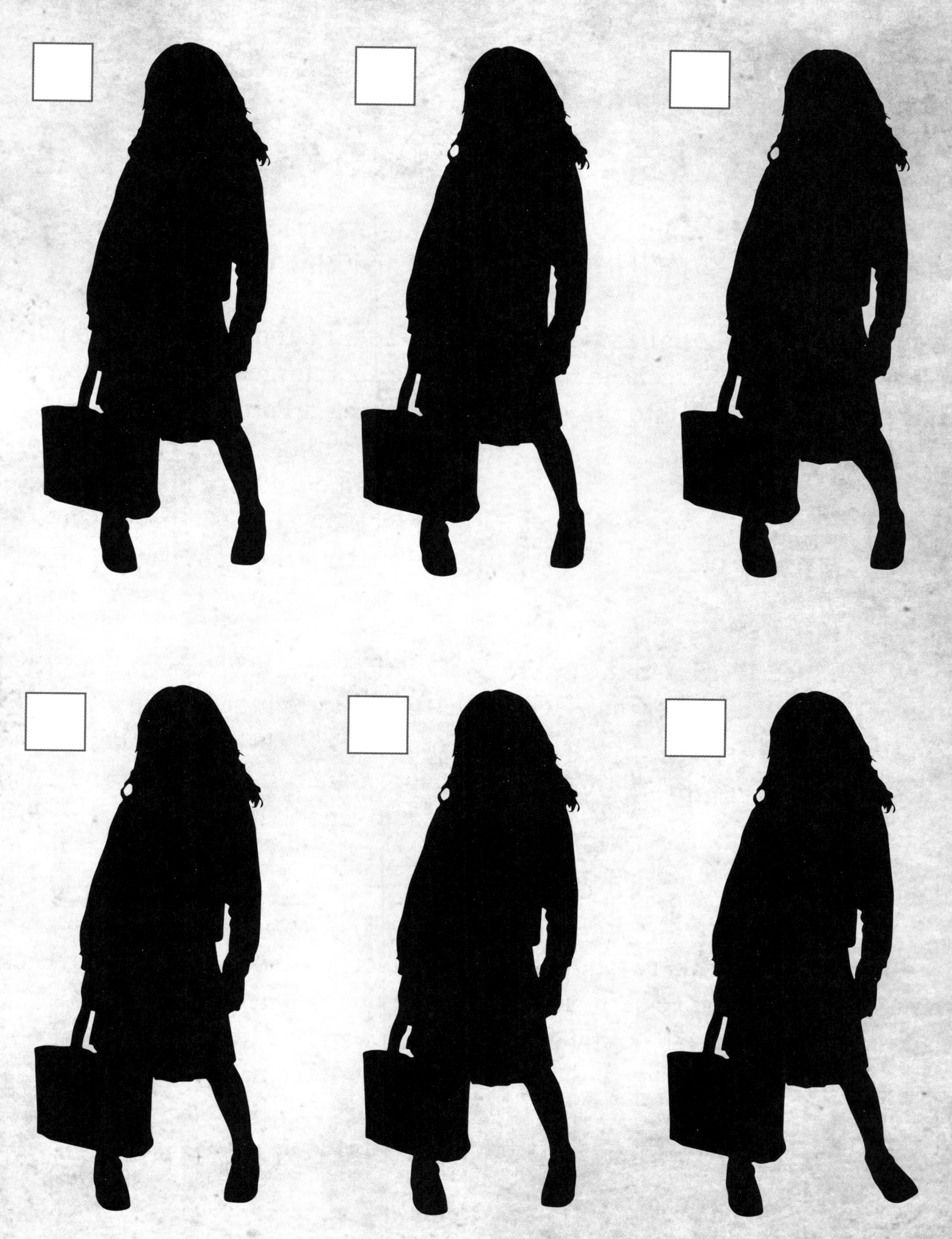

Hogwarts Curriculum: Year 2

How closely were you paying attention to the *Harry Potter* books and films?

1. How many Ford Anglias were destroyed to film the scene in which Harry and Ron crash into the Whomping Willow?
A. 14
B. 10
C. 4
D. 7

2. Which special effect in the *CoS* film was practical rather than CGI?
A. Tom Riddle's diary
B. The door to the Chamber of Secrets
C. The rogue bludger
D. Dobby

3. There is a rumor that Dobby the house-elf's appearance in the films is based on this Russian politician:

_______ _________

4. Tom Felton improvised which line upon forgetting the correct one?
A. "Scared Potter?"
B. "Training for the ballet, Potter?"
C. "Famous Harry Potter can't even go into a bookshop without making the front page."
D. "I didn't know you could read."

5. A perceptive viewer may notice this important item from *Half-Blood Prince* actually makes its first appearance in the Borgin and Burkes set in Knockturn Alley.

_________ _________

6. Who was originally cast as Gilderoy Lockhart but had to back out due to scheduling conflicts?
A. Ewan McGregor
B. Hugh Grant
C. Christian Bale
D. Jude Law

Rupert Grint as Ron Weasley in *Harry Potter and the Chamber of Secrets* (2002).

Hogwarts Curriculum: Year 2

How closely were you paying attention to the Harry Potter books and films?

7. The faux title used to disguise the set by the crew was this Bruce Springsteen song:
A. "Glory Days"
B. "Tougher Than the Rest"
C. "Incident on 57th Street"
D. "Brilliant Disguise"

8. What are the seven ingredients of Polyjuice potion?

____________ ____________
____________ ____________
____________ ____________
____

9. This defensive charm, which causes an opponent to release whatever they are holding, was learned in the book's inaugural Dueling Club meeting.

____

10. Hermione used this spell to freeze the pixies Lockhart unleashed on his second-year class in the book.

____

11. In the book, Harry uses this spell on Malfoy to induce tickling during their duel. ___________

12. After Malfoy summons a snake in the book by shouting _____during Dueling Club, Harry's Parseltongue abilities are revealed when he tells the snake to back off of Justin Finch-Fletchley.

COLLECTION CHRISTOPHEL/ALAMY

Miriam Margolyes as Professor Sprout in *Harry Potter and the Chamber of Secrets* (2002).

Hogwarts Curriculum: Year 2

How closely were you paying attention
to the *Harry Potter* books and films?

13. In the book, Hermione uses _______ on Tom Riddle's diary in an attempt to reveal invisible ink. Unfortunately this revealing charm does not work.

14. This spell was used by Snape to vanish the snake summoned by Malfoy during his duel with Harry in the book. _______ _______

15. This spell was used to blast away acromantulas in order to save Ron and Harry from Aragog's children in the film. __________ _________

16. ________ _______ is a counter spell for general use and terminates all spell effects. It is used by Snape during a particularly chaotic Dueling Club practice in the book.

17. Can you fill in the blanks in Ginny's valentine's poem to Harry?
"His eyes are as green as a fresh _____ ______,
His ____ is as dark as a blackboard.
I wish he was ____, he's truly divine,
the hero who conquered the ____ ____."

18. Which of the following appeared at Nearly Headless Nick's Deathday Party in the book?

A. Maggoty haggis
B. Moldy cake
C. Rotten deviled eggs
D. Fungus-covered peanuts
E. Chains for the ghosts to shake at their leisure
F. A ghost orchestra featuring a musical saw
G. Dull gray candles
H. A gray cake shaped like a tombstone

Tom Felton as Draco Malfoy in *Harry Potter and the Chamber of Secrets* (2002).

Are You a Quidditch Expert?

If you can spot the fake Quidditch rules, you're a star Seeker.

1. Chasers can pass the ball between each other but only one is allowed to enter into the scoring zone at any one time.

REAL FAKE

2. The winner of the match is the team that finds the Golden Snitch.

REAL FAKE

3. Contact is allowed, but a player may not seize hold of another player's broomstick or any part of their anatomy.

REAL FAKE

4. There is no time limit to a Quidditch game; it goes on until the Snitch is found.

REAL FAKE

5. During a penalty shot, though the Keeper maintains their position near the goals, any player may block an incoming shot on goal.

REAL FAKE

6. If any member of the crowd casts a spell on a player, the benefitting team forfeits the game.

REAL FAKE

7. If any player leaves the boundaries of the field, they surrender the Quaffle to the other team.

REAL FAKE

8. Any player on the team may call time outs, which may be extended to two hours if a game has already lasted for more than 12 hours.

REAL FAKE

BONUS During the Quidditch World Cup of 1473, every foul in the Quidditch rule book was committed. How many are there?

____

Tom Felton as Draco Malfoy in *Harry Potter and the Chamber of Secrets* (2002).

The Slytherin and Gryffindor Slytherin teams in uniform for their match in *Harry Potter and the Chamber of Secrets* (2002).

Match Day Logic

Use logic and locate the Golden Snitch to help Harry defeat Slytherin on the pitch.

IT'S GRYFFINDOR VS. SLYTHERIN, the most hotly contested Quidditch match of the year at Hogwarts. From their position on the field, Gryffindor's Seeker notices that the players and Quidditch balls in their view are arranged in a grid. What's more, they've just spotted the Snitch! Using the clues on the opposite page, can you fill in the blank grid and reveal its location?

FROM LEFT: PICTURELUX/THE HOLLYWOOD ARCHIVE/ALAMY TK; SHUTTERSTOCK

IN VIEW

Gryffindor Players

Katie Bell
Angelina Johnson
Alicia Spinnet
Fred Weasley
George Weasley

Slytherin Players

Marcus Flint
Draco Malfoy
Adrian Pucey

Quidditch Balls

Bludger #1
Bludger #2
Quaffle
Snitch

CLUES

1. Angelina Johnson is two spaces below Alicia Spinnet, who is two spaces to the left of Draco Malfoy, who is immediately above Bludger #2.
2. Fred Weasley is directly to the right of Bludger #1, which is two spaces below Adrian Pucey.
3. Adrian Pucey is two spaces to the right of George Weasley.
4. The Golden Snitch is below Marcus Flint, who is two spaces to the left of Katie Bell.

Slytherin's basilisk is attacked by Fawkes the phoenix in *Harry Potter and the Chamber of Secrets* (2002).

Enemies Of The Heir Beware

Can you match the five means of petrification to the six students and Hogwarts dwellers who met the gaze of the basilisk?

FROM LEFT: WARNER BROS/MOVIESTILLSDB; TCD/PROD.DB/ALAMY

1. Mrs. Norris __

2. Colin Creevey __

3. Nearly Headless Nick __

4. Justin Finch-Fletchley __

5. Hermione Granger __

6. Penelope Clearwater __

A. Saw the basilisk's reflection in a hand mirror.

B. Saw the basilisk through a camera lens.

C. Saw the basilisk's reflection in a puddle caused by the flooding in the nearby bathroom.

D. Saw the basilisk through a ghost.

E. Looked the basilisk straight in the eye.

Daniel Radcliffe as Harry Potter in *Harry Potter and the Chamber of Secrets* (2002).

Teacher of the Year

1. How many of his own books does Lockhart assign as textbooks for his class?
A. 3
B. 7
C. 1
D. 10

2. How many works did Lockhart publish in total? __________

3. How many times did Lockhart win *Witch Weekly*'s Most Charming Smile Award?
A. 4
B. 3
C. 7
D. 5

4. What is Lockhart's favorite color?
A. Lilac
B. Lavender
C. Periwinkle
D. Violet

5. Which house was Lockhart in as a student?
____

6. Though Lockhart didn't actually take part in any of the feats detailed in his novels, at which charm was he most accomplished that helped him take credit for those deeds?
A. Vanishing Spell
B. Switching Spell
C. Memory Charm
D. Banishing Charm

7. Which spell does Lockhart use to try to immobilize the pixies he unleashes on his class?
A. *Partis Temporus*
B. *Peskipiksi Pesternomi*
C. *Piertotum Locomotor*
D. *Periculum*

8. How many points does Hermione earn for Gryffindor with a perfect score on Lockhart's biographical quiz?
A. 5
B. 100
C. 10
D. 20

9. Lockhart is an honorary member of which organization?
A. Auror Office
B. Dark Force Defense League
C. Order of the Phoenix
D. Order of Merlin

ALBUM/ALAMY

Professor Lockhart

Kenneth Branagh as Gilderoy Lockhart in *Harry Potter and the Chamber of Secrets* (2002).

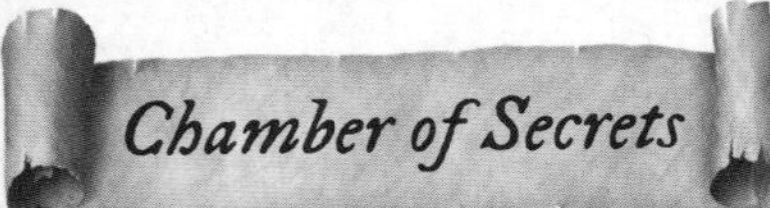

Gilderoy In Print

Which are the real Gilderoy Lockhart titles hiding among the impostors?

Daniel Radcliffe as Harry Potter and Kenneth Branagh as Gilderoy Lockhart in *Harry Potter and the Chamber of Secrets* (2002).

A
BREAK WITH A BANSHEE

B
HIKING WITH HIPPOGRIFFS

C
GADDING WITH GHOULS

D
KNEADING WITH KNEAZLES

E
GNASHING WITH GNOMES

F
LEARNING WITH LEPRECHAUNS

G
HOLIDAYS WITH HAGS

H
DUSTING WITH DOXIES

I
TRAVELS WITH TROLLS

J
VOYAGES WITH VEELA

K
WALTZING WITH WEREWOLVES

L
YEAR WITH THE YETI

M
DANCING WITH DRAGONS

N
MARAUDING WITH MONSTERS

The Right Stuff

Can you follow the correct path to a successful Polyjuice Potion?

Add fluxweed and knotgrass to your cauldron, stir four times clockwise.

Wave your wand over it and let brew for 60–80 minutes.

Add the piece of your subject along with boomslang skin, stir clockwise once.

Let sit at high heat for 60 minutes before adding leeches and knotgrass.

Add the piece of your subject, along with another scoop of crushed lacewings and turn up the heat.

Add lacewings to your cauldron, stir once counterclockwise.

Wave your wand and let sit for 30 minutes.

Make a mixture of fluxweed and bicorn horn, let sit for 1,440 minutes.

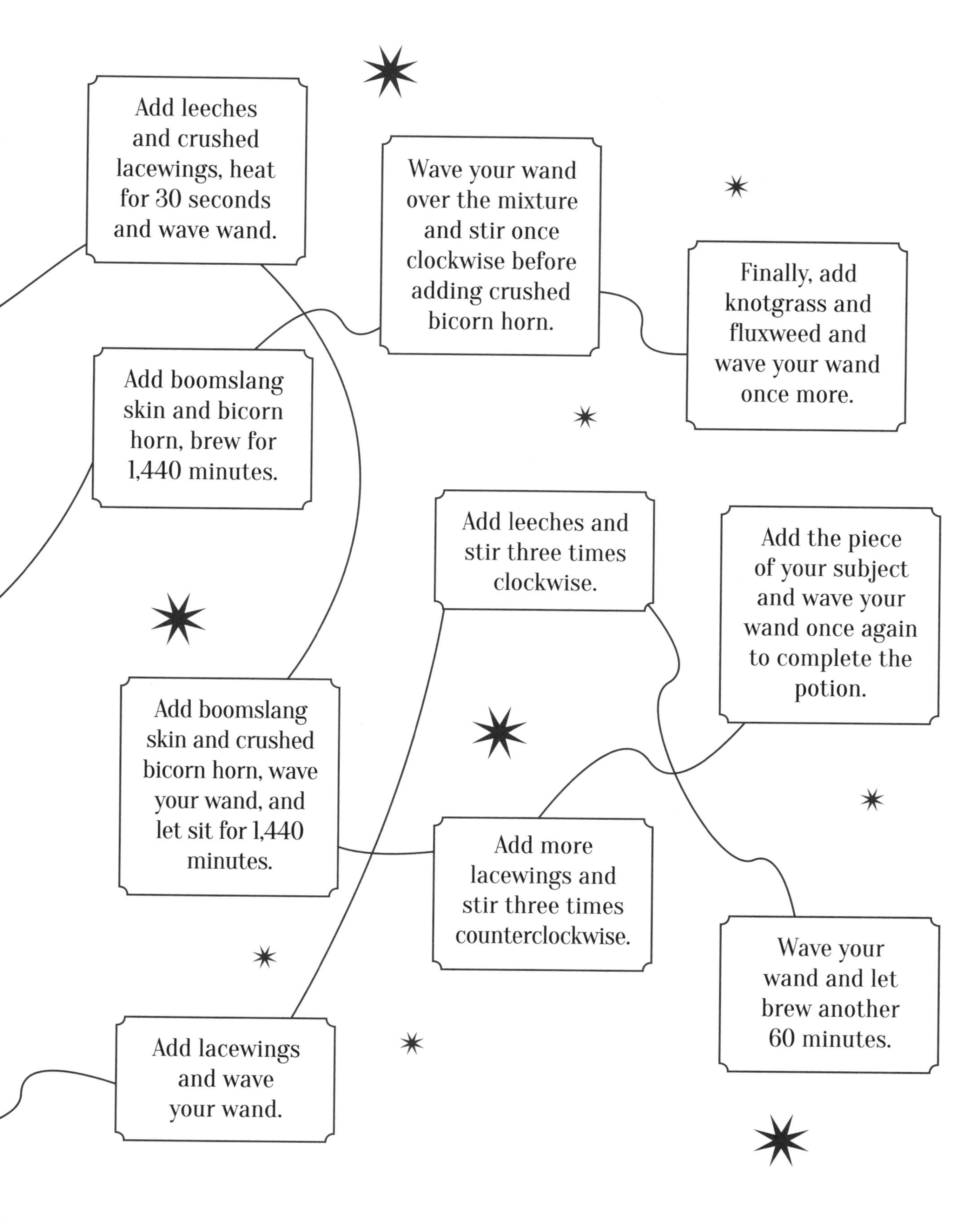
Add leeches and crushed lacewings, heat for 30 seconds and wave wand.
Wave your wand over the mixture and stir once clockwise before adding crushed bicorn horn.
Finally, add knotgrass and fluxweed and wave your wand once more.
Add boomslang skin and bicorn horn, brew for 1,440 minutes.
Add leeches and stir three times clockwise.
Add the piece of your subject and wave your wand once again to complete the potion.
Add boomslang skin and crushed bicorn horn, wave your wand, and let sit for 1,440 minutes.
Add more lacewings and stir three times counterclockwise.
Wave your wand and let brew another 60 minutes.
Add lacewings and wave your wand.

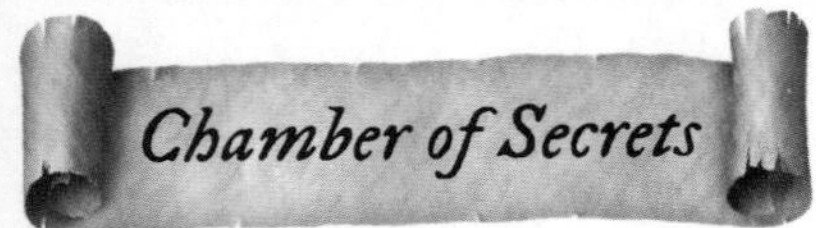

MuggleNet's Expert Trivia: Year 2

You must have been paying close attention to every word of the saga if you can answer all of these questions.

1. Born to a Muggle father and witch mother, this professor was the only one of his siblings to display magical abilities.

____

2. On a scale of X to XXXXX, what is the Ministry of Magic classification for a Niffler?

____

3. Caretaker Argus Filch claims there is a list of how many forbidden items available for perusal in his office?

____

4. How many total chapters, including the epilogue, are there in the *Harry Potter* series?

____

Owl post arrives at the Gryffindor table in *Harry Potter and the Chamber of Secrets* (2002).

Weasleys' Wizarding Clock

Determine which Weasley should go in each hand of the clock based on the description.

1. **GETS** in a fight with a Malfoy in Flourish and Blotts
2. **HAD** their prefect badge bewitched to read "Pinhead"
3. **ACCIDENTALLY** places their arm in a butter dish at The Burrow
4. **WORKS** at Gringotts in Egypt
5. **WORKS** with dragons in Romania

1

2

3

4

5

FROM LEFT: SHUTTERSTOCK; WARNER BROS/MOVIESTILLSDB

...deroy Lockhart book to complete a task at home

6.CONS...

7.DRIVES the Flying Ford Anglia to save Harry from the Dursleys

8.RECEIVES a Howler in the Great Hall

9.PICKS the lock to the cupboard under the stairs to get Harry's Hogwarts supplies

Julie Walters as Molly Weasley and Mark Williams as Arthur Weasley.

Harry Potter and the Prisoner of Azkaban

As Harry returns to Hogwarts for his third year, a wanted criminal is on the loose. But how dangerous is he really?

ALBUM/ALAMY

Did You Know?

Harry's Pocket Sneakoscope continually goes off throughout the year due to the presence of Peter Pettigrew in the Gryffindor boys' dormitory.

Alan Rickman as Severus Snape, Rupert Grint as Ron Weasley, Emma Watson as Hermione Granger and Daniel Radcliffe as Harry Potter in *Harry Potter and the Prisoner of Azkaban* (2004).

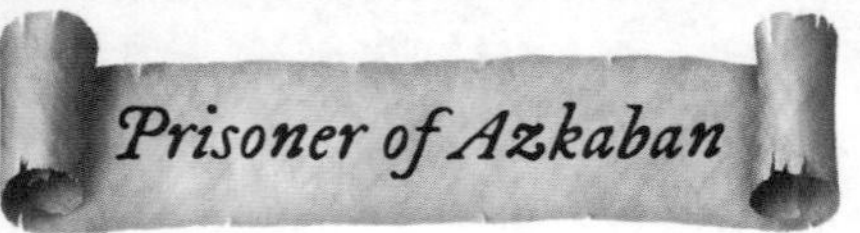

Fill-In-The Blanks

After accidentally blowing up his ____ ________ like a weather balloon, Harry runs away from 4 __________ _______ and makes his way to Diagon Alley with the help of the triple-decker _____ ____. As he whiles away the time on the wizarding world's most famous street, he has no idea he's in grave danger: ________ ______, the most notorious Death Eater in the wizarding prison ________, has escaped. Upon arriving at Hogwarts, Harry learns this fugitive was responsible for the deaths of his _________, and the adults in his life—especially the new DADA teacher, _______ ______— are determined to protect him, which he sees as little more than being babied. Unable to leave the castle, Harry nevertheless sneaks out with the help of the _________'s _____, given to him by ___ and _______. The story of Azkaban's famous escapee is more complicated than it seems, however, and it's soon revealed that ______ ________, who has been hiding out as Ron's pet rat ________, was actually the one who betrayed Harry's family. Though still on the run from the law, ________ becomes a friend and godfather to Harry.

PICTURELUX/THE HOLLYWOOD ARCHIVE/ALAMY

Rupert Grint as Ron Weasley, Emma Watson as Hermione Granger and Daniel Radcliffe as Harry Potter in *Harry Potter and the Prisoner of Azkaban* (2004).

Gary Oldman as Sirius Black in *Harry Potter and the Prisoner of Azkaban* (2004).

Escape From Azkaban

Sirius Black is about to change into his Animagus form to sneak past the Dementors. Can you help him find his way out safely?

START

END

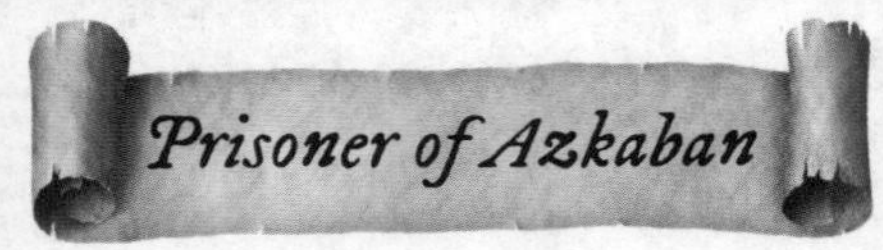

Hogwarts Curriculum: Year 3

How closely were you paying attention to the *Harry Potter* books and films?

1. What assignment did Alfonso Cuarón give to Daniel Radcliffe, Rupert Grint and Emma Watson before filming began?
A. Read *Prisoner of Azkaban*
B. Write essays about their characters
C. Both A and B

2. There's an Easter egg on the Marauder's Map the first time Harry opens it in the film. Whose name is shown?
A. Newt Scamander
B. Peter Pettigrew
C. Richard Harris

3. What does Cuarón establish in the *Harry Potter* universe that will continue throughout the rest of the films?
A. Modern-day, casual wardrobes for the students
B. The castle's layout
C. Both A and B

4. Of the three characters below, who appears in the movie but has no lines?
A. Parvati Patil
B. Percy Weasley
C. Dudley Dursley

5. In the film, the scene where Harry learns the Patronus charm was originally going to take place in...
A. The Slytherin Common Room
B. The Room of Requirement
C. Dumbledore's office

6. What are the names of the cats who portrayed Crookshanks in the film?
A. Pumpkin and Crackerjack
B. Fluffy and Ginger
C. Muffin and Chester

Emma Thompson as Sybill Trelawney in *Harry Potter and the Prisoner of Azkaban* (2004).

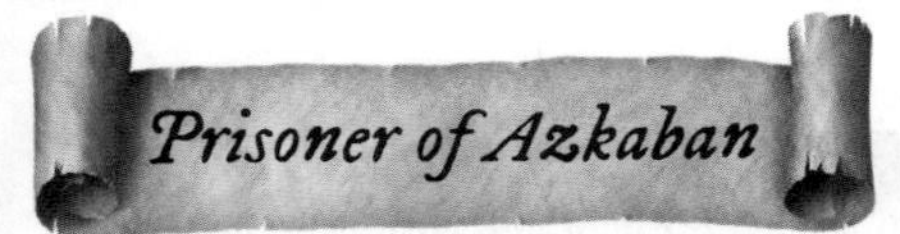

Hogwarts Curriculum: Year 3

How closely were you paying attention to the *Harry Potter* books and films?

7. When Harry arrives at the Leaky Cauldron in the film, a wizard is using magic to stir his mug. What muggle book is he reading?

____

8. The incantation __________ creates a dazzling light at the end of the wand, enabling the witch or wizard to see in the dark.

9. The charm ______ repels a boggart, but the word is not enough. _____ finishes it off.

10. In the movie, what spell does Hermione use to free Sirius from Dumbledore's office?

____

11. What doesn't the Patronus charm project?
A. Happiness
B. Hope
C. Despair
D. The need to survive

Daniel Radcliffe as Harry Potter with Buckbeak the hippogriff in *Harry Potter and the Prisoner of Azkaban* (2004).

David Thewlis as Remus Lupin in *Harry Potter and the Prisoner of Azkaban* (2004).

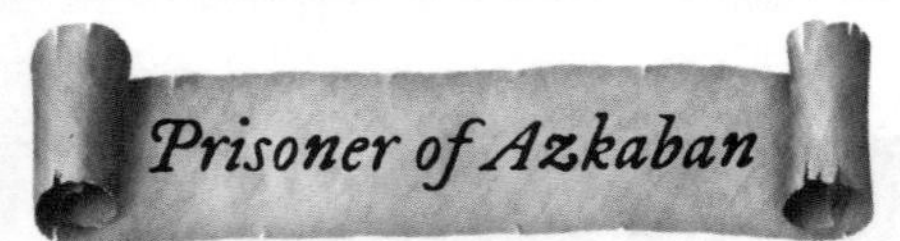

Hogwarts Curriculum: Year 3

How closely were you paying attention to the *Harry Potter* books and films?

12. When Peeves the Poltergeist blocks a keyhole with gum in the book, Professor Lupin teaches his class a spell, ______, that shoots the gum up Peeves's left nostril.
A. *Mimblewimble*
B. *Entomorphis*
C. *Waddiwasi*
D. *Terego*

13. In the book, Hermione uses __________ on Harry's glasses so he can see in the stormy conditions in the match against Hufflepuff.

14. What's the spell that opens up hidden passageways?
A. *Dissendium*
B. *Alohomora*
C. *Evanesco*
D. *Obscuro*

15. During his Charms exam in the book, Harry accidentally overdoes the ______ Charm and causes Ron to laugh uncontrollably.

16. In the book, Dumbledore says the incantation _______ ________ to stop Harry from smashing into the ground after falling off his broom.

Tom Felton as Draco Malfoy in *Harry Potter and the Prisoner of Azkaban* (2004).

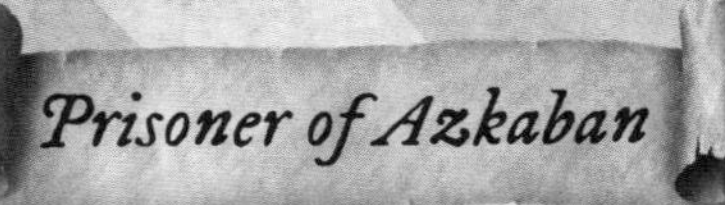

Magic Shadows

Can you tell which of the silhouettes opposite is a direct match?

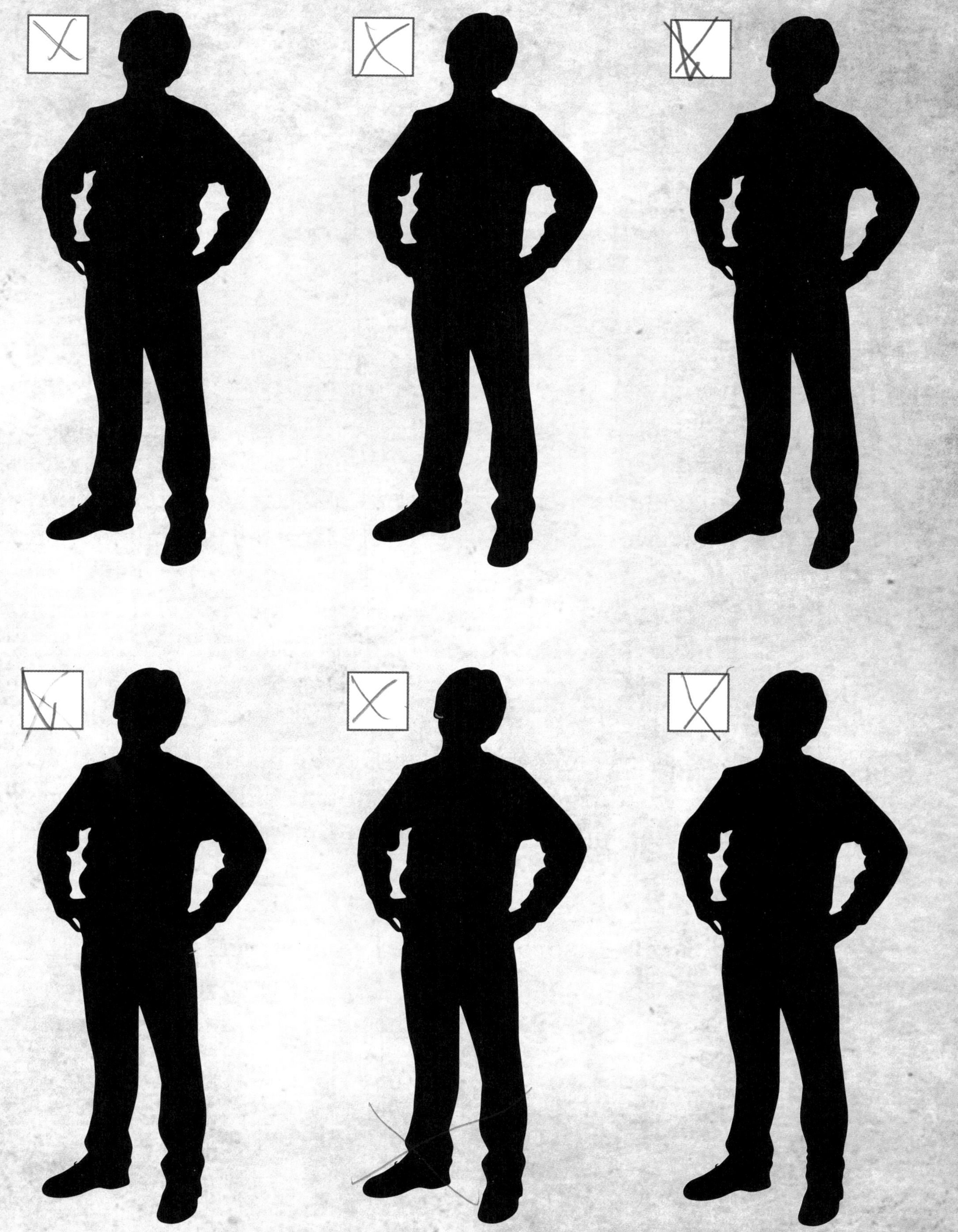

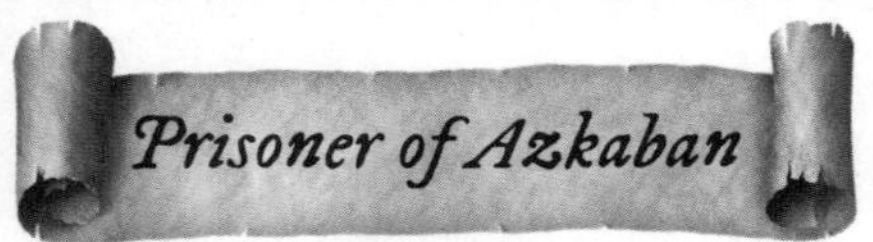

Teacher of the Year

1. What dark creatures do the third years study in Lupin's class?
A. Boggarts, Hinkypunks, Redcaps, Kappas, Grindylows
B. Boggarts, Hinkypunks, Redcaps, Grindylows, Werewolves
C. Boggarts, Hinkypunks, Redcaps, Grindylows, Dementors
D. Boggarts, Hinkypunks, Redcaps, Grindylows, Vampires

2. When Snape takes over Lupin's class while he's ill, what page does Snape demand the class turn to?

____

3. Who knows about Professor Lupin's secret before he reunites with Sirius in the Shrieking Shack?
A. Madam Pomfrey
B. Hermione
C. Malfoy
D. A and B

4. Professor Lupin's boggart turns into a ____ ____ when he faces it.

5. Why does Sirius recommend Pettigrew as the Potters' Secret-Keeper instead of Lupin?
A. Sirius didn't want to be it.
B. Sirius thought Lupin was the spy.
C. Lupin couldn't be a Secret-Keeper because he is a werewolf.

6. During his fifth year, Lupin's friends become _____ ______ so they can help him during the full moon.

7. Lupin forgets to say "_______ _____" after spotting Pettigrew on the map, allowing _____ to use it.

David Thewlis as Professor Lupin in *Harry Potter and the Prisoner of Azkaban* (2004).

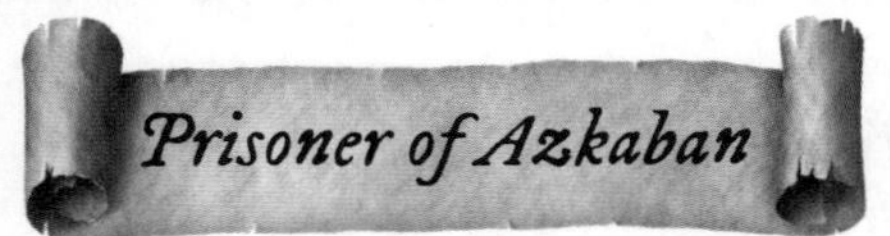

Hogsmeade Village

Can you unscramble the Hogsmeade landmarks seen or visited by Harry and friends?

1. VESDIRH DAN ABGENS

2. HTE O'HGS EHDA

3. HNOEDKSUYE

4. HSGEMOEDA TSATNOI

5. ZKON'OS JEKO HSPO

6. EHT HSRNIKEIG SAHKC

7. TEH TEREH KOBROMSICST

8. SHOMEGEDA TOSP FOFCIE

9. MDAMA PDUDFOTIO'S TAE OHPS

Did You Know?

Moody may be one of the only people to have ever seen a boggart's natural form, because of his magical eye.

HELEN NICHOLSON/ALAMY

At Universal Orlando Resort's Islands of Adventure theme park, guests can mail letters from the Owl Post office (pictured) and visit re-imaginings of other Hogsmeade landmarks.

Hagrid's Care of Magical Creatures Quiz

Do you remember Hagrid's first year of teaching well enough to pass his class?

1. Who was the Care of Magical Creatures professor before Hagrid?
A. Professor Grubbly-Plank
B. Professor Burbage
C. Professor Kettleburn

2. Who helps Hagrid prepare Buckbeak's defense for the trial and appeal?
A. Harry, Ron and Hermione
B. Ron and Hermione
C. Hermione

3. The book Hagrid assigns is called ______________________.

4. In the book, how many hippogriffs does Hagrid show the class?
A. 5
B. 12
C. 3

5. The class's flobberworms die because they had too much __________.

Daniel Radcliffe as Harry Potter with Buckbeak the hippogriff in *Harry Potter and the Prisoner of Azkaban* (2004).

Care of Magical Creatures

Harry and his classmates begin their studies of Care of Magical Creatures in third year. Can you unscramble the creature in their curriculum and match it to its description?

Robbie Coltrane as Hagrid, Emma Watson as Hermione Granger, Rupert Grint as Ron Weasley and Daniel Radcliffe as Harry Potter in *Harry Potter and the Prisoner of Azkaban* (2004).

BSALT-NEEDD KSERTW ________________	Not to be confused with the magic-less animal of the same name, a fire-starting lizard.
FHPOPIIRFG ________________	An objectively boring, herbivorous animal Draco Malfoy claims to have been bitten by.
LOWBMERBORF ________________	A creature created by Hagrid by cross-breeding fire crabs with manticores.
SLADAMAREN ________________	A creature with magical blood and a single horn on its forehead.
INLFEFR ________________	A horse-like creature invisible to those who have not witnessed death.
TEHTRALS ________________	An eagle-horse hybrid that proves essential to a *Prisoner of Azkaban* escape plan.
NUCORIN ________________	A creature obsessed with shiny objects that becomes a main character in the *Fantastic Beasts* films.

Monster Book of Word Jumbles

Can you unscramble the animals that can be found in the infamous Care of Magical Creatures textbook?

HAGRID'S ADDITION to the Care of Magical Creatures curriculum, *The Monster Book of Monsters*, has a habit of shredding anything in its path if it's not soothed with a tickle on the spine. That, unfortunately, includes one unlucky student's notes. They've been torn to shreds! Can you put the pieces back together in order, revealing the relevant magical beasts?

___ ___ ___ ___ ___ ___ ___

ALBUM/ALAMY

X O D Y   P A P K A

___ ___ ___ ___   ___ ___ ___ ___ ___

U N N U D

___ ___ ___ ___ ___

A W C I D L I R

___ ___ ___ ___ ___ ___ ___ ___

G R A T G O B

___ ___ ___ ___ ___ ___ ___

W U C K B O L E R T

___ ___ ___ ___ ___ ___ ___ ___ ___ ___

R O E W O P F

___ ___ ___ ___ ___ ___ ___

I M E G S E D U I

___ ___ ___ ___ ___ ___ ___ ___ ___

P O G H A R N R

___ ___ ___ ___ ___ ___ ___ ___

Oliver and James Phelps as the Weasley Twins.

The Jinxed Gobstone

The Hogwarts Gobstones Club has been pranked! Can you help them discover which of their marbles has been jinxed?

SOMEONE HAS PLAYED a prank on the oft-maligned Hogwarts Gobstones Club, filling one of their stones with a potent new acne-inflamer from Weasleys' Wizard Wheezes that'll give them a barbershop quartet of huge singing forehead pimples. The good news is that the contaminated marble weighs a scant half a gram more than the normal ones. Snape has lent them a two-pan scale from his supplies but will only allow them to make two measurements before he takes it back. He claims that's more than enough to figure out which marble is contaminated. How can you use the scale in two measurements to determine which of the eight Gobstones in the bag has been jinxed? Remember, you only have two weighings to narrow it down.

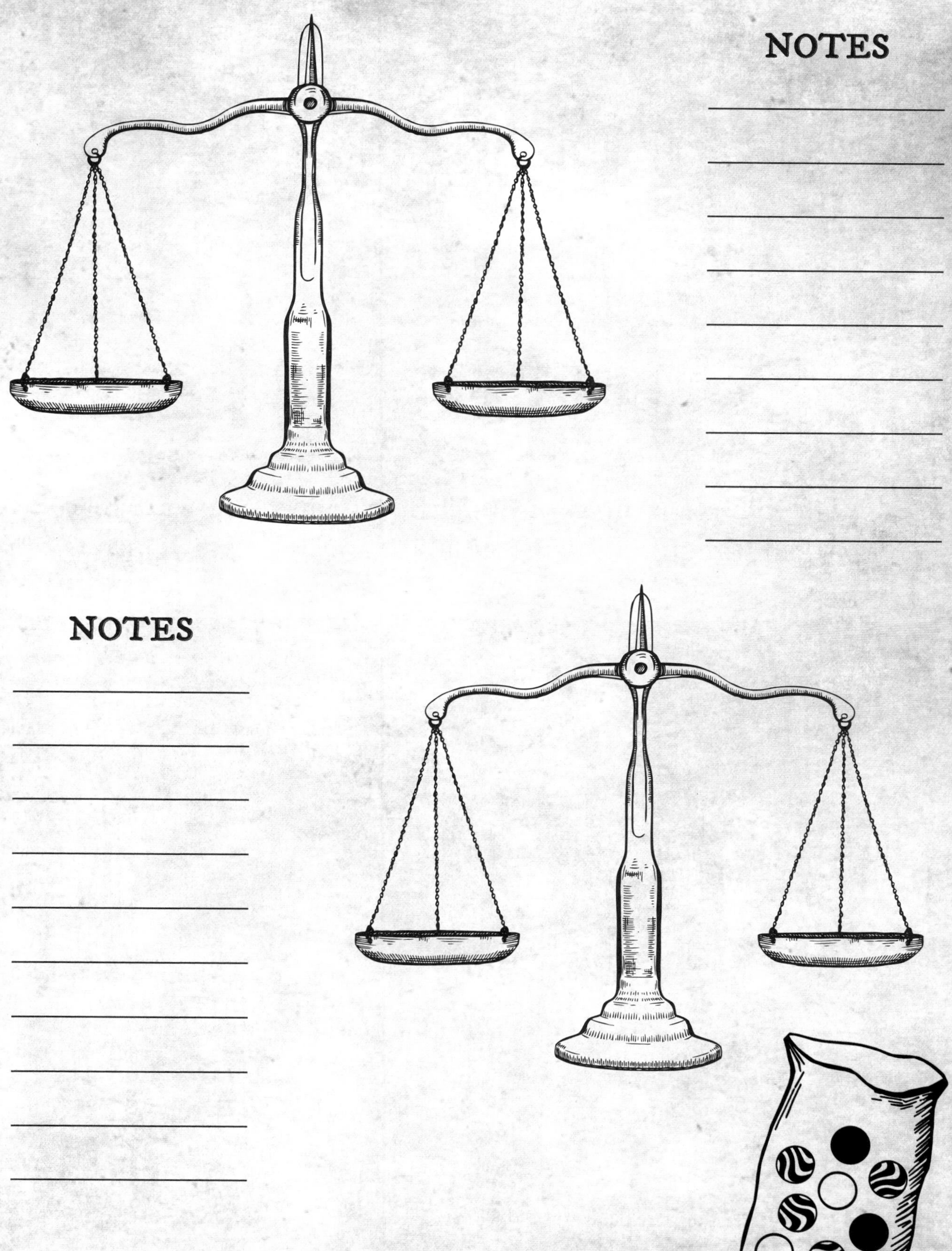

NOTES

NOTES

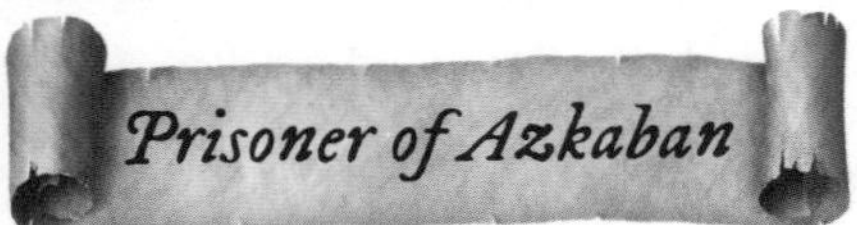

Hermione's Impossible Schedule

Can you name the subjects in Hermione's schedule, so packed it required the manipulation of time and space?

Emma Watson as Hermione Granger and Daniel Radcliffe as Harry Potter in *Harry Potter and the Prisoner of Azkaban* (2004).

PICTURELUX/THE HOLLYWOOD ARCHIVE/ALAMY

______________________, Professor Snape

______________________, Professor Lupin

______________________, Hagrid

______________________, Professor Vector

______________________, Professor Trelawney

______________________, Professor Burbage

______________________, Professor Sprout

______________________, Professor McGonagall

______________________, Professor Flitwick

______________________, Professor Babbling

______________________, Professor Binns

______________________, Professor Sinistra

Prisoner of Azkaban

The Eye of the Seer

Professor Sybill Trelawney introduces Harry and his fellow third years to the imprecise art of Divination. Test your memory and determine whether these statements are true or false.

1. Trelawney predicted Neville would break his tea cup on the first day of Divination.

2. She told Lavender the thing she dreaded most would come to pass on September 16.

3. Trelawney warned the class one of their number would leave them forever around June.

4. During Christmas dinner, Trelawney says the first person to leave the table of 13 will die, and she ends up being correct.

5. She told Padma Patil to "beware a red-headed man."

6. When Trelawney finally makes a true prediction about Voldemort reuniting with his servant, she doesn't believe it to be true.

7. Trelawney's classroom is located in the North Tower on the seventh floor.

8. She sees the Grim in Harry's tea leaves and the Crystal Ball.

Emma Thompson as Sybill Trelawney in *Harry Potter and the Prisoner of Azkaban* (2004).

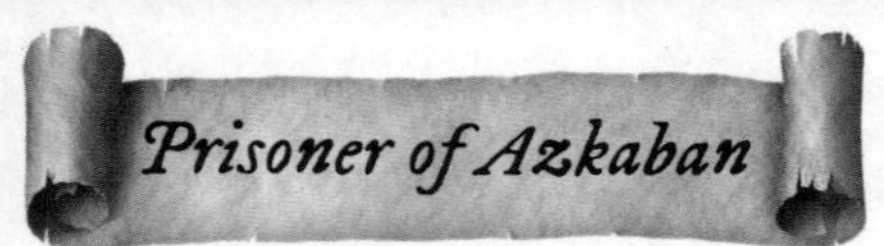

MuggleNet's Expert Trivia: Year 3

You must have been paying close attention to every word of the saga if you can answer all of these questions.

1. What is Harry's room number in Diagon Alley when he stays prior to starting his third year at Hogwarts?

____

2. How many beds are on each level of the Knight Bus?

____

3. What is the difference between male and female Blast-Ended Skrewts?

____

4. Who was McGonagall's first love?

____

Maggie Smith as Minerva McGonagall in *Harry Potter and the Prisoner of Azkaban* (2004).

The Marauder's Map

After solemnly swearing one is up to no good, Hogwarts and the surrounding environs become easier to navigate than Hogsmeade's High Street. Can you fill in the blanks?

Ciarán Hinds as Aberforth Dumbledore, Rupert Grint as Ron Weasley and Emma Watson as Hermione Granger in *Harry Potter and the Deathly Hallows: Part 2* (2011).

1. ______

In *Harry Potter and the Deathly Hallows*, the Hog's Head re-supplies

The first passage used by Harry in the books and films gets him to Hogsmeade.

Sirius suggests that this passage might be big enough

Lupin's werewolf hideaway

HONEYDUKES

HONEYDUKES · HOMEMADE SWEETS

Honeydukes sweet shop at Universal Orlando Resort's Islands of Adventure theme park.

2. ______ VILLAGE

3. ______

Gary Oldman as Sirius Black in *Harry Potter and the Prisoner of Azkaban* (2004).

CLOCKWISE FROM TOP RIGHT: WARNER BROS/MOVIESTILLSDB (2); WARNER BROS/EVERETT COLLECTION; WARNER BROS/MOVIESTILLSDB; STEPHEN SEARLE/ALAMY; PICTURELUX/THE HOLLYWOOD ARCHIVE/ALAMY

Tom Felton as Draco Malfoy in *Harry Potter and the Half-Blood Prince* (2009).

Hogwarts Castle and the Whomping Willow as seen in *Harry Potter and the Prisoner of Azkaban* (2004).

David Bradley as Argus Filch in *Harry Potter and the Prisoner of Azkaban* (2004).

ARGUS FILCH's 3 SECRET PASSAGES

When Fred and George give Harry the map, they specify three passages that are still intact but unfortunately known to Argus Filch, the caretaker, which means his feline spy, Mrs. Norris, could be lurking in any of them waiting to catch a student out of line.

Harry Potter and the Goblet of Fire

Harry's fourth year at Hogwarts is also the year the wizarding world changes forever.

Did You Know?

This book is one of four (the others being *Sorcerer's Stone*, *Half-Blood Prince* and *Deathly Hallows*) that open with chapters that aren't from Harry's point of view.

Michael Gambon as Albus Dumbledore in *Harry Potter and the Goblet of Fire* (2005).

Fill-In-The-Blanks

Shortly before his fourth year at Hogwarts begins, Harry and his pals are treated to a trip to the Quidditch ________ _____, at which the _______ and __________ teams vie for the top prize in the sport. During the ensuing celebrations, however, a spell is cast that illuminates the night sky with ____ _______ ______, a symbol of the Dark wizard Voldemort. His followers seem to be back and are becoming more bold. Hogwarts, in response, hires ___-_____ ________ as the new Defense Against the Dark Arts professor. His unorthodox style is, however, a clue that something is seriously wrong. Witches and wizards from all over the world are excited to learn that the ancient ___________ Tournament, featuring champions from Europe's three most prestigious magic academies (_______, _______ and _________), will be held again this year. But when a fourth name emerges from the magical ________ ___ ______ that announces the champions, it's none other than Harry Potter's. Risking his life to complete three magical tasks alongside fellow champions ______ ________, _______ _________ and ______ ________, Harry soon discovers his involvement in the tournament was a ruse orchestrated by Voldemort. When he grips the handle of the tournament's trophy, he is transported to a graveyard where Voldemort and his loyal servant, ________ ___________, are waiting. With the help of love and magic, he escapes once more, but the world is dramatically changed: Voldemort is back.

Emma Watson as Hermione Granger, Rupert Grint as Ron Weasley and Daniel Radcliffe as Harry Potter in *Harry Potter and the Goblet of Fire* (2005).

Diagon Alley Mix-Up

Can you fix the magically mixed-up image?

1 2 3 4

F

E

D

C

B

A

A MISCHIEVOUS POLTERGEIST fond of haunting the *Daily Prophet*'s offices has magically split this image of Diagon Alley into pieces and rotated or flipped 12 of them. Can you pick out which ones have been altered (and how) to help fix the image?

RICHART PHOTOS/ALAMY

The Quidditch World Cup

How well do you recall the match?

1. What's the name of the magical binoculars Harry buys for himself, Ron and Hermione?
A. Omnioculars
B. Unioculars
C. Owloculars

2. Ludo Bagman is the head of ________.
A. Magical Law Enforcement
B. Magical Games and Sports
C. International Magical Cooperation

3. Which one of these players is not on the Bulgarian team?
A. Vulchanov
B. Zograf
C. Dragomir

4. How much money do the Weasley twins bet Bagman that Ireland will win, but Bulgaria will catch the snitch?
A. 35 Gallons, 15 Sickles and 3 Knuts
B. 37 Gallons, 15 Sickles and 3 Knuts
C. 37 Gallons, 15 Sickles and 4 Knuts

5. Which one of these players is not on the Ireland team?
A. Quigley
B. Murphy
C. Mullet

6. Why is Barty Crouch's absence so notable?
A. His elf, Winky, is saving a seat for him
B. Fudge expected Crouch to help with the Bulgarian Minister
C. Both A and B

7. Viktor Krum's signature move, which he uses against Irish Seeker Lynch, is the ______ ______.

8. Mr. Weasley advises the boys to ______ ______ ____ to avoid becoming entranced by the Veela.

9. The final score of the World Cup is Ireland _____, Bulgaria ____.

Emma Watson as Hermione Granger, Daniel Radcliffe as Harry Potter and Rupert Grint as Ron Weasley in *Harry Potter and the Goblet of Fire* (2005).

The Championship Teams

At right are listed the rosters of the Irish and Bulgarian national Quidditch teams. Can you spot the three fake names on each team?

Did You Know?

After Harry sends the food package to Sirius, he sees an eagle owl with a note in its beak soar past Hagrid's hut toward the castle. That eagle owl was carrying Voldemort's order to Barty Crouch Jr. that he should stop Barty Crouch Sr., who had escaped, at all costs.

Stanislav Yanevski as Viktor Krum.

FROM LEFT: WARNER BROS/MOVIESTILLSDB; SHUTTERSTOCK

IRELAND	BULGARIA
MULLET	DIMITROV
MORAN	IVANOVA
TROY	ZHUKOV
McGILLICUDDY	KORNOVA
O'HARA	LEVSKI
CONNOLLY	VULCHANOV
RYAN	VOLKOV
QUIGLEY	KRUM
LYNCH	ZOGRAF
O'BRIAN	NABOKOV

FOR BONUS HOUSE POINTS

Professional Teams of Britain and Ireland

Can you prove your seeking skills and match the locations with their pro Quidditch team's name?

Kestrels	Falcons	Arrows
Wasps	Pride	Catapults
Cannons	Magpies	Tornados
United	Harpies	
Wanderers	Bats	

1. Ballycastle ________
2. Puddlemere ________
3. Montrose ________
4. Kenmare ________
5. Tutshill ________
6. ______ of Portree
7. Appleby ________
8. Caerphilly ________
9. Holyhead ________
10. Wimbourne ________
11. Chudley ________
12. Wigtown ________
13. Falmouth ________

FROM LEFT: SHUTTERSTOCK; PICTURELUX/THE HOLLYWOOD ARCHIVE/ALAMY

Daniel Radcliffe as Harry Potter in *Harry Potter and the Chamber of Secrets* (2002).

Hogwarts Curriculum: Year 4

How closely were you paying attention to the *Harry Potter* books and films?

1. Daniel Radcliffe's costars got to practice the Yule Ball dance routine for three weeks. How much time did he get?
A. Four days
B. Four months
C. One week

2. Members of which English bands made up the Weird Sisters in the film?
A. The Rolling Stones and Led Zeppelin
B. Pulp and Radiohead
C. Pulp and Blur

3. Which of these characters appeared in the movie?
A. Winky
B. Ludo Bagman
C. Walden Macnair

4. During the graveyard scene in the film, the names of Voldemort's paternal grandparents are revealed, though they are never mentioned in the book. What are they?
A. Thomas Riddle Sr. and Patricia Riddle
B. Thomas Riddle Sr. and Jane Riddle
C. Thomas Riddle Sr. and Mary Riddle

5. This is the first film in the franchise to...
A. Not feature Molly Weasley
B. Star Richard Harris as Dumbledore
C. Be directed by David Yates

Matthew Lewis as Neville Longbottom, Daniel Radcliffe as Harry Potter, Devon Murray as Seamus Finnegan and James Phelps as Fred Weasley in *Harry Potter and the Goblet of Fire* (2005).

Hogwarts Curriculum: Year 4

How closely were you paying attention to
the *Harry Potter* books and films?

6. How much time did Daniel Radcliffe have to spend underwater shooting the second task?

____

7. In the book, Harry uses the incantation ______, which he learned in Flitwick's Charms class, to summon his Firebolt in the first task.

8. The ______ ______ is the opposite of the Summoning Charm.

9. Used most frequently in the books by Ludo Bagman, _____ is a charm that amplifies the witch or wizard's voice.

10. ______ is an incantation Death Eaters use to conjure the Dark Mark.

David Tennant as Barty Crouch, Jr. in *Harry Potter and the Goblet of Fire* (2005).

Hogwarts Curriculum: Year 4

How closely were you paying attention to the *Harry Potter* books and films?

11. The incantation _____ is often used in combat and renders the person it hits semi- or unconscious.

12. The _____ Curse blasts obstacles apart.

13. Both Fleur and Cedric use the _____ -_____ Charm in the second task, which allowed them to survive underwater.

14. In the book, Harry used the incantation ________ to slow down Hagrid's Blast-Ended Skrewt in the maze.

15. The _______ spell causes the caster's wand to turn into a compass and point North.

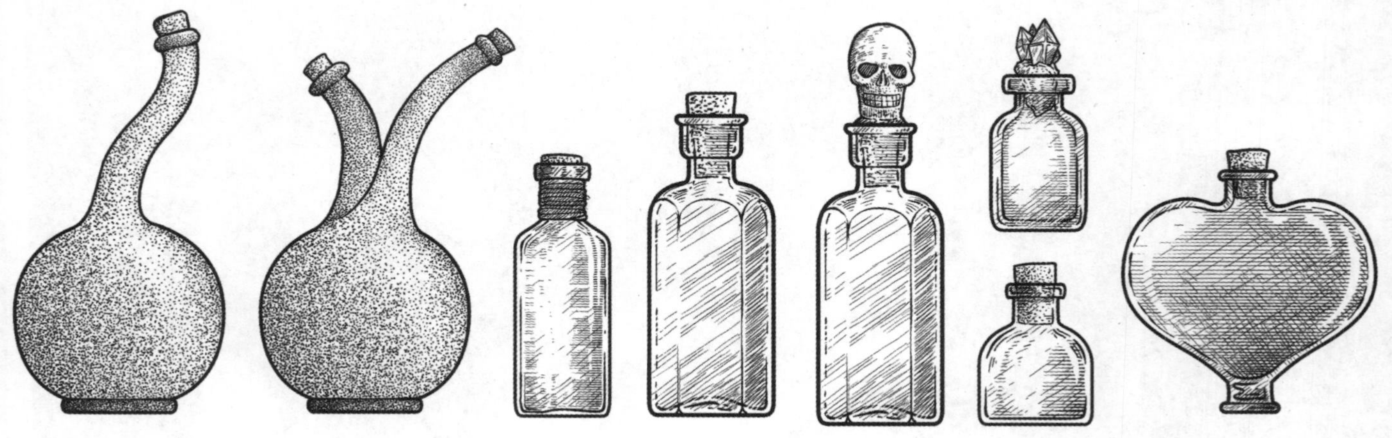

FROM LEFT: SHUTTERSTOCK; WARNER BROS/EVERETT COLLECTION

Emma Watson as Hermione Granger and Daniel Radcliffe as Harry Potter in *Harry Potter and the Goblet of Fire* (2005).

Goblet of Fire

The World of Wizarding Schools

Though Harry Potter's story takes place largely at Hogwarts, there are wizarding stories taking place at schools all over the world. Can you place these schools where they belong on the map?

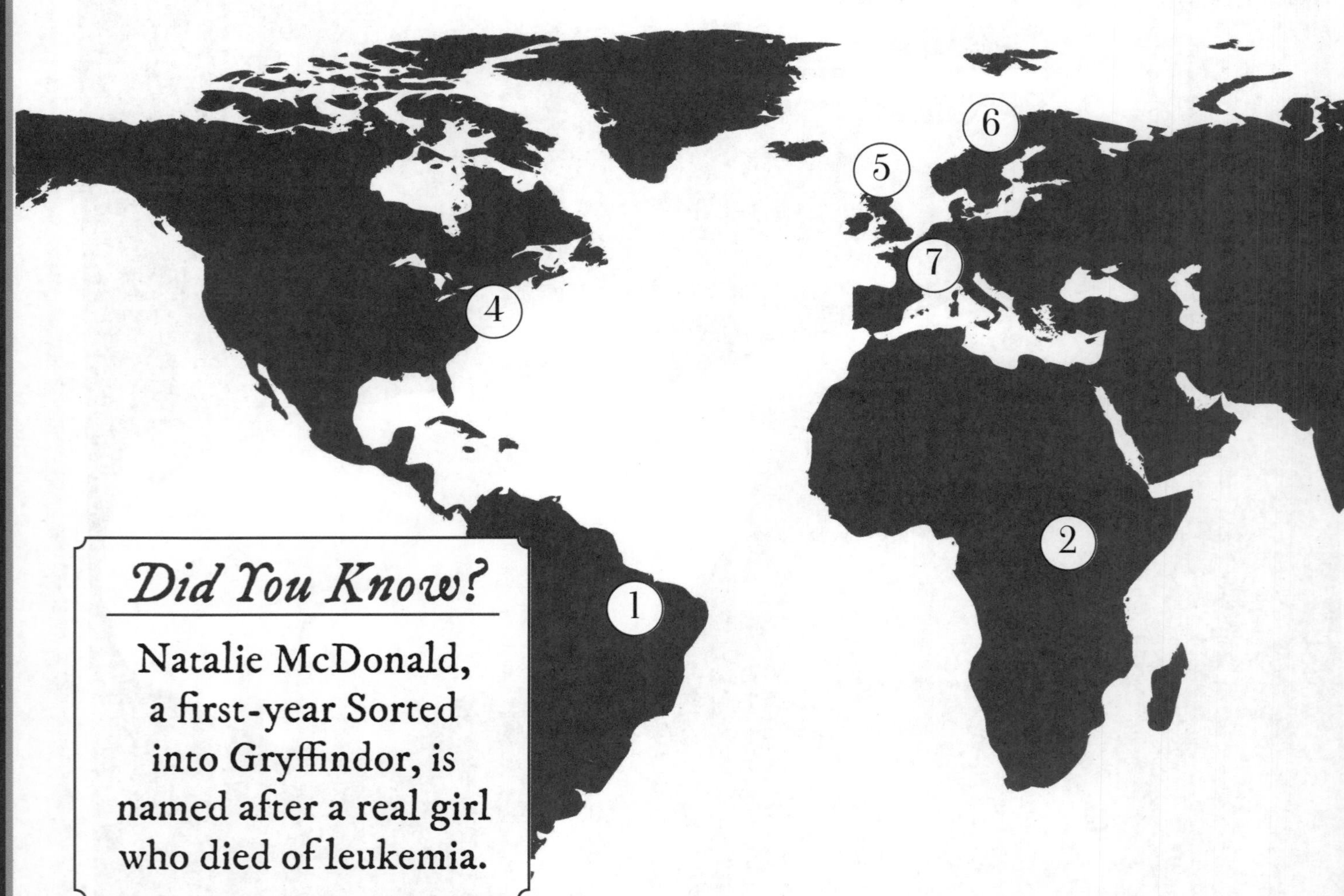

Did You Know?

Natalie McDonald, a first-year Sorted into Gryffindor, is named after a real girl who died of leukemia.

1. A golden edifice in the Brazilian rainforest that appears to be a ruin to Muggles, just like Hogwarts.

____

2. Though smaller wizarding schools exist throughout Africa, this school draws students from every country on the continent. It is the largest wizarding school in the world.

____

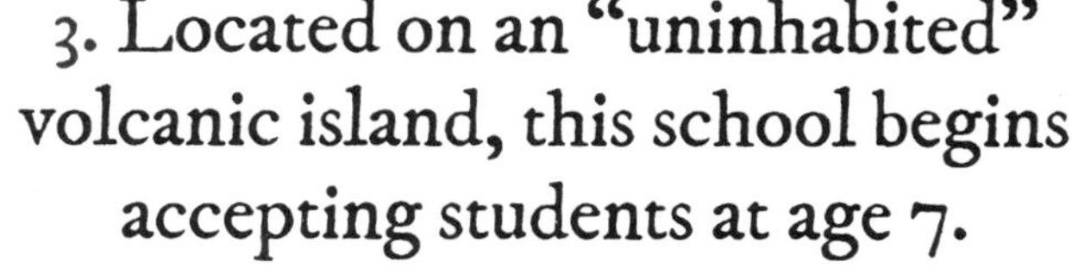

3. Located on an "uninhabited" volcanic island, this school begins accepting students at age 7.

____

4. The North American wizarding school, modeled after Hogwarts, can be found at Mount Greylock in Massachusetts.

____

5. Hidden in the Scottish Highlands is this school, which serves as the main setting for the *Harry Potter* saga, and the first one to be set on paper by J.K. Rowling.

____

6. It is largely Gellert Grindelwald's having attended the school that gives this northern European institution its dark reputation.

____

7. The French wizarding academy can be found somewhere in the Pyrenees Mountains and is also the alma mater of Nicolas Flamel.

____

Goblet of Fire

The Yule Ball

Can you match the characters in the columns below with their dates to the dance?

Harry Potter	Neville Longbottom
Ron Weasley	Angelina Johnson
Hermione Granger	Parvati Patil
Cedric Diggory	Roger Davies
Ginny Weasley	Viktor Krum
Fleur Delacour	Padma Patil
Seamus Finnigan	Lavender Brown
Fred Weasley	Cho Chang

Alan Rickman as Severus Snape, Maggie Smith as Minerva McGonagall and Michael Gambon as Albus Dumbledore in *Harry Potter and the Goblet of Fire* (2005).

Daniel Radcliffe as Harry Potter and Rupert Grint as Ron Weasley in *Harry Potter and the Goblet of Fire* (2005).

Teacher of the Year

1. Mad-Eye Moody lost a chunk of his nose fighting the Death Eater ____________.

2. What can Moody's magical eye see through?
A. Invisibility cloaks
B. Solid objects
C. Both A and B

3. What does Professor McGonagall reprimand Moody for?
A. Casting Unforgivable Curses on students
B. Using Transfiguration as a punishment
C. Helping Harry with the second task

4. How does Barty Crouch Jr. break free from his father's imprisonment?
A. He throws off the Imperius Curse
B. Peter Pettigrew and Voldemort find him
C. He kills his father

5. Disguised as Mad-Eye, Barty Crouch Jr. suggests that Harry become a(n) _______ after Hogwarts.

6. When does Dumbledore realize Professor Moody is an impostor?
A. After he asks to take the Cup into the maze
B. After he takes Harry back to the castle
C. When the Polyjuice Potion wears off

7. The real Moody is revealed to be hidden in his own ____ and under the ______ Curse.

Professor Moody

Brendan Gleeson as Alastor Moody in *Harry Potter and the Goblet of Fire* (2005).

The Triwizard Tournament

Facing dragons, grindylows and Sphinxes, the four champions are up against dangerous obstacles. See how well you remember the Tournament.

THE FIRST TASK

1. On which date does the first task take place?
A. October 31
B. November 16
C. November 24

2. Cedric turns a _____ into a ____ to try to get his dragon to go for it instead.

3. What score does Karkaroff give Harry?
A. 1
B. 3
C. 4

THE SECOND TASK

1. In the book, who gives Harry the gillyweed minutes before the second task?
A. Neville
B. Dobby
C. Moody

2. Harry earns _____ points in the second task, tying with ____ _____.

3. Harry brings ___ _____ and ______ _____ up from the lake.

THE THIRD TASK

1. What's the first obstacle Harry encounters in the maze?
A. The Sphinx
B. Blast-Ended Skrewt
C. Boggart

2. The answer to the Sphinx's riddle is "______."

3. As Harry and Cedric both grab the Triwizard Cup, they realize it's a ________.

Daniel Radcliffe as Harry Potter in *Harry Potter and the Goblet of Fire* (2005).

The Triwizard Maze

Can you find your way to the center of the maze before the other Triwizard champions?

Start

WARNER BROS/EVERETT COLLECTION

Robert Pattinson as Cedric Diggory in *Harry Potter and the Goblet of Fire* (2005).

Voldemort Returns

Take this quiz to see how well you remember that fateful night in the graveyard.

1. The ingredients of Voldemort's resurrection were:
A. Bone of the father, willingly given; flesh of the servant, unwillingly given; and blood of the enemy, forcibly taken.
B. Bone of the father, forcibly taken; flesh of the servant, willingly given; and blood of the enemy, willingly given.
C. Bone of the father,unknowingly given; flesh of the servant, willingly given; and blood of the enemy, forcibly taken.

2. What color does the potion turn after all the ingredients and Voldemort are added?
A. Red
B. Green
C. White

3. Peter Pettigrew helps Voldemort return to a rudimentary body in the beginning of *Goblet of Fire* with a few spells, a couple unspeakable acts and a potion of _____ blood and ____ venom from ______.

4. Harry throws off the _______ _____ and refuses to ___ to Voldemort before their duel.

5. Which Death Eater(s) missed Voldemort's rebirthing party?
A. Nott
B. The Lestranges
C. Crabbe Sr. and Goyle Sr.

6. Who unwittingly helped Voldemort reunite with his most faithful servant?
A. Frank Bryce
B. Barty Crouch Jr.
C. Bertha Jorkins

7. When Harry makes his last stand against Voldemort, he meets the Killing Curse with the incantation ____________.

8. Who is the fourth person to appear out of Voldemort's wand during *Priori Incantatem*?
A. Lily Potter
B. James Potter
C. Bertha Jorkins

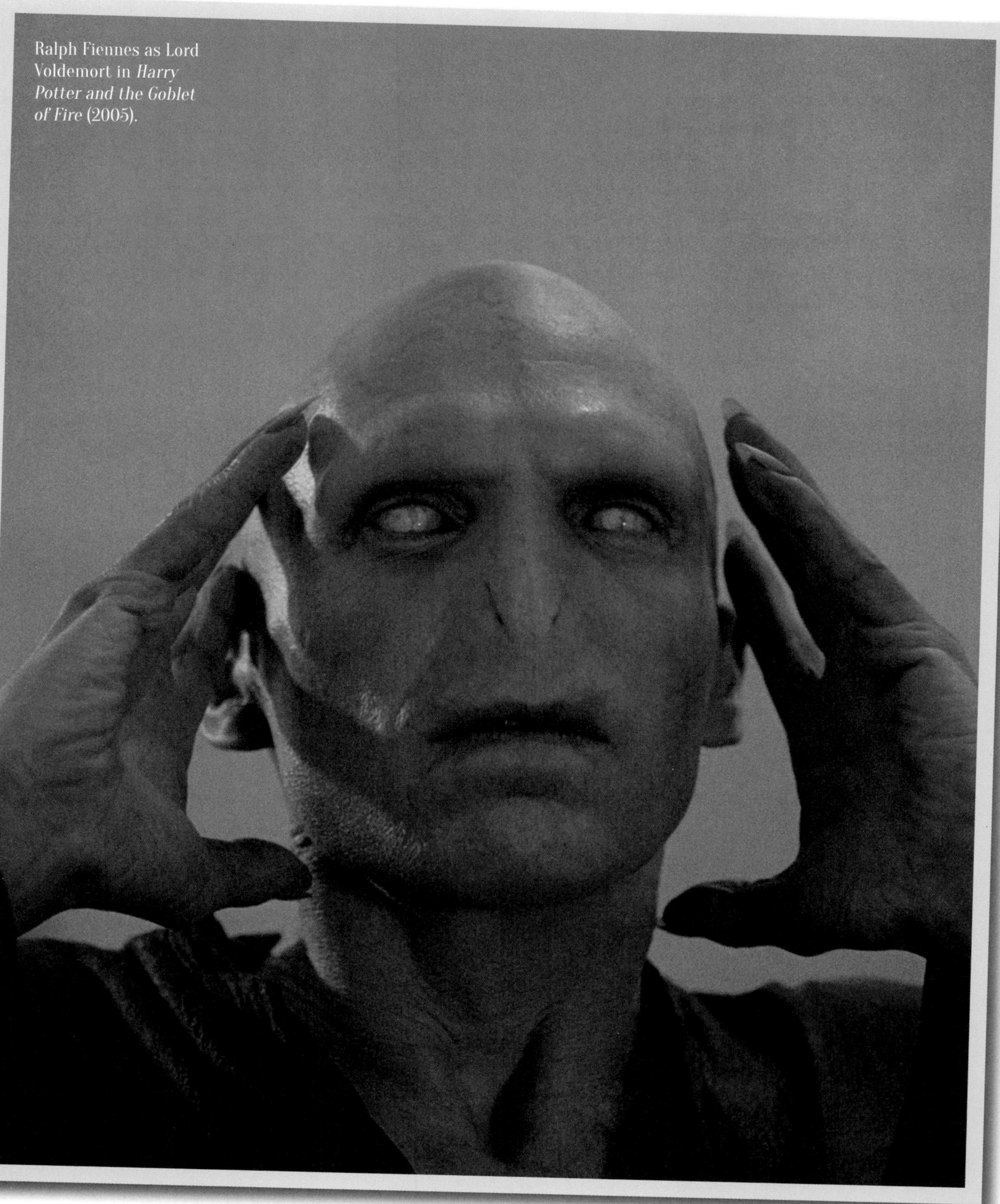

Ralph Fiennes as Lord Voldemort in *Harry Potter and the Goblet of Fire* (2005).

MuggleNet's Expert Trivia: Year 4

You must have been paying close attention to every word of the saga if you can answer all of these questions.

1. Bathilda Bagshot sends an owl to Dumbledore after being impressed by his article on what topic in *Transfiguration Today*?

____

2. Name this professor's wand: 10 and a quarter, cypress tree, unicorn hair, pliable

____

3. With the front half of a horse and the back end of the fish, this creature shares a name with a part of the human brain.

____

4. Herpo the Foul created the first what?

____

Michael Gambon as Albus Dumbledore in *Harry Potter and the Goblet of Fire* (2005).

Harry Potter and the Order of the Phoenix

Voldemort is back, but the wizarding world refuses to believe it, as Harry prepares for his O.W.L.s.

Dumbledore's Army infiltrates the Ministry of Magic in search of Professor Trelawney's prophecy in *Harry Potter and the Order of the Phoenix* (2007).

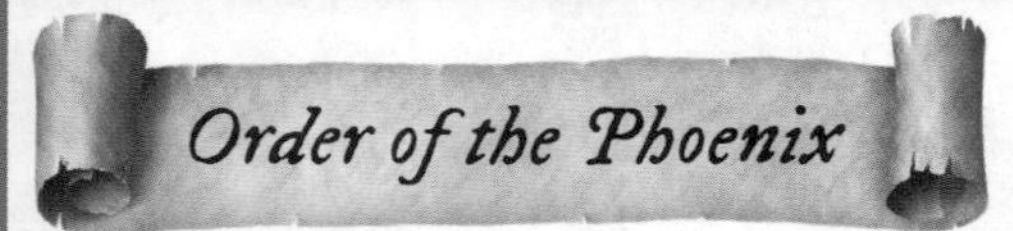

Fill-In-The-Blanks

After the events of *Harry Potter and the Goblet of Fire*, it's clear to Harry, his friends and the ever-loyal headmaster ________ __________ that Voldemort has returned and is preparing to make war on the wizarding world. The only problem? The Minister of Magic, ______ ______, and the cowardly toadies at his side won't admit anything is wrong. Meanwhile, Harry, Ron and Hermione learn about a secret organization, the titular _________ ___ ____ _________, that was on the front lines of the fight against the ______ _________ more than a decade ago. Including the Weasleys, Harry's godfather _____ ______, Remus Lupin and his soon-to-be love interest ________ _______, this group makes their headquarters at ___ _________ ______. At Hogwarts, Harry is instructed in the art of keeping others out of your thoughts—______________, for those with wizarding vocabularies—by Professor ________. But his distrust of the teacher proves a massive mistake when Voldemort lures Harry and his friends to the __________ ___ _______. Here, a massive battle ensues, as Harry looks for a __________ regarding his relationship to the Dark Lord. The events of this skirmish will help the wizarding world at large to accept Voldemort's return, but for Harry this comes at a terrible price, the loss of ______.

Gary Oldman as Sirius Black and Daniel Radcliffe as Harry Potter in *Harry Potter and the Order of the Phoenix* (2007).

Lost in Muggle London

Can you help an absent-minded Muggle Studies student find his way to the Portkey home?

THE N.E.W.T.-LEVEL MUGGLE STUDIES students at Hogwarts have been assigned a bit of fieldwork over their holiday break: visiting the British Museum for the day and submitting two scrolls of parchment on an artifact of their choosing. One particularly absent-minded member of the class has been so caught up in exploring the museum he's lost track of time and is about to miss the Portkey that will take him back to Godric's Hollow, where he's spending the holiday with friends. He's not quite sure where the Portkey is, but he's just noticed another student from his group rushing out the door. Using the map of London provided, can you follow in their footsteps and reveal the location of the Portkey home?

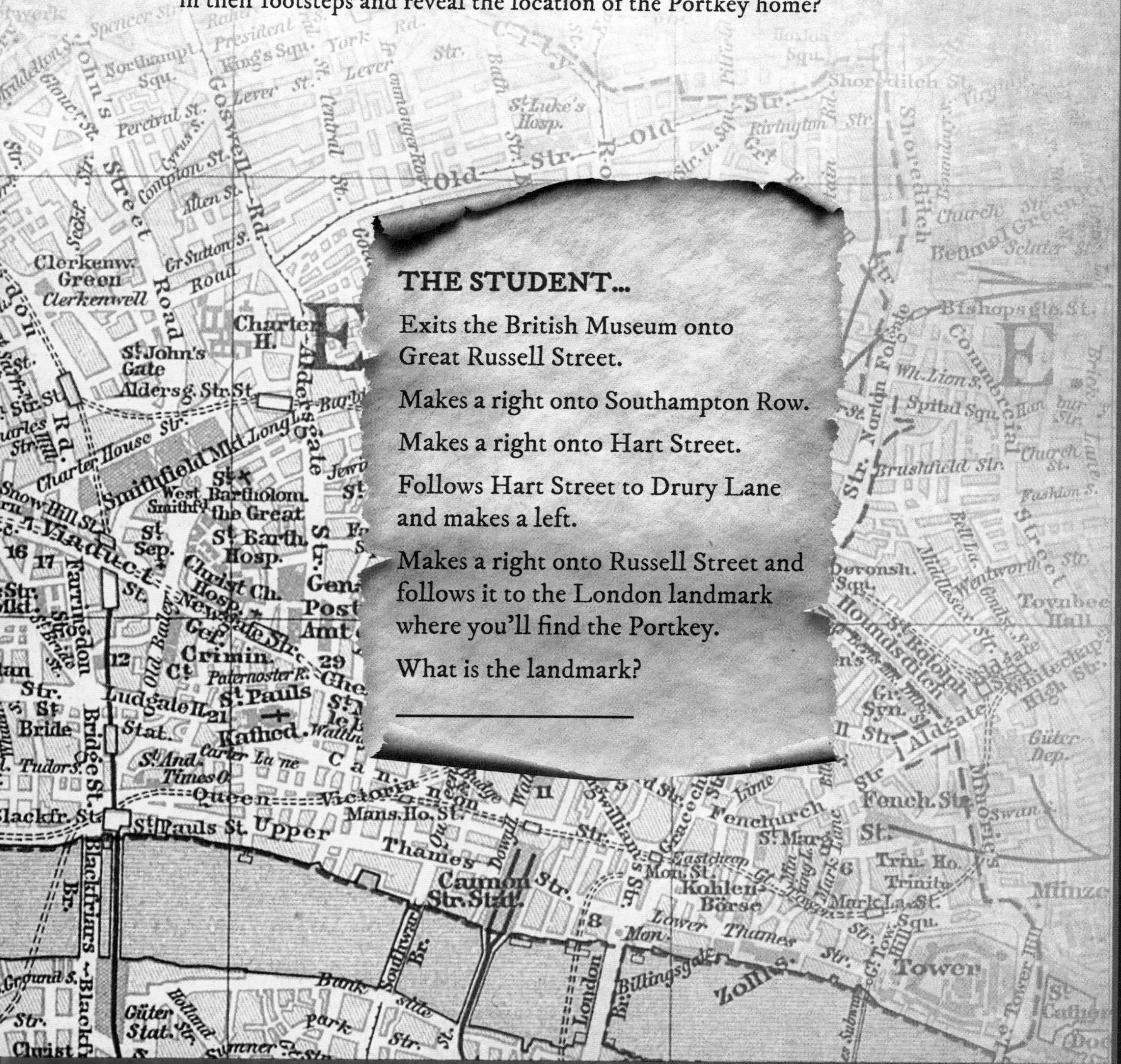

THE STUDENT...

Exits the British Museum onto Great Russell Street.

Makes a right onto Southampton Row.

Makes a right onto Hart Street.

Follows Hart Street to Drury Lane and makes a left.

Makes a right onto Russell Street and follows it to the London landmark where you'll find the Portkey.

What is the landmark?

____

Your O.W.L. Exams: Year 5

Use your comprehensive knowledge from the past five years at Hogwarts to see if you can master this expert-level grab bag of wizarding knowledge.

1. A _____ _____ is used to swap two different objects for one another.
A. Swapping Spell
B. Switching Spell
C. Switch Charm
D. Trading Spell

2. What is the result of the incantation *Flintifors*?
A. Turns a desk into a pig
B. Turns a rabbit into a slipper
C. Turns a small creature or item into a matchbox
D. Turns a small creature or item into a snuffbox

3. The incantation _____ _____ transforms an animal into a goblet.
A. *Vera Verto*
B. *Ventus Duo*
C. *Verdimillious Duo*
D. *Vulnera Sanentur*

4. Holding a mandrake leaf in one's mouth for a month and reciting a specific incantation on a daily basis is part of the process of:
A. Becoming an Animagus
B. Keeping your human mind during werewolf transformations
C. Becoming a Metamorphmagus
D. Permanently changing one's hair color

5. What is the incantation for the Bird-Conjuring Charm?
A. *Avifors*
B. *Anteoculatia*
C. *Anapneo*
D. *Avis*

6. The incantation *Evanesco*:
A. Causes the target to grow in size
B. Transforms the target into an insectoid for a short time
C. Vanishes both animate and inanimate objects
D. Adheres one object to another

Hogwarts students sit for their exams in the Great Hall, rearranged from its usual four-table setup.

Your O.W.L. Exams: Year 5

Use your comprehensive knowledge from the past five years at Hogwarts to see if you can master this expert-level grab bag of wizarding knowledge.

7. Monkshood and wolfsbane are also known as:
A. Wormwood
B. Aconite
C. Asphodel
D. Moondew

8. Approximately how long does it take to brew a Polyjuice Potion?
A. Three months
B. Two weeks
C. One month
D. Two months

9. A ______ _______ is used to soothe a person after experiencing shock, trauma or an emotional outburst.
A. Soothing Solution
B. Calming Draught
C. Draught of Peace
D. Girding Potion

10. Name the four lessons Snape taught his students in Year 5 (that we know of):
(1) ____________________
(2) ____________________
(3) ____________________
(4) ____________________

11. Which potion does Snape brew for Professor Lupin during Harry's third year at Hogwarts?
A. Wolfsbane Potion
B. Wormwood Potion
C. Wiggenweld Potion
D. Strengthening Solution

12. What is the best incantation to use against a boggart?
A. *Ridiculous*
B. *Riddikulus*
C. *Ridonkulous*
D. *Ridiklis*

Hogwarts students amass in the courtyard.

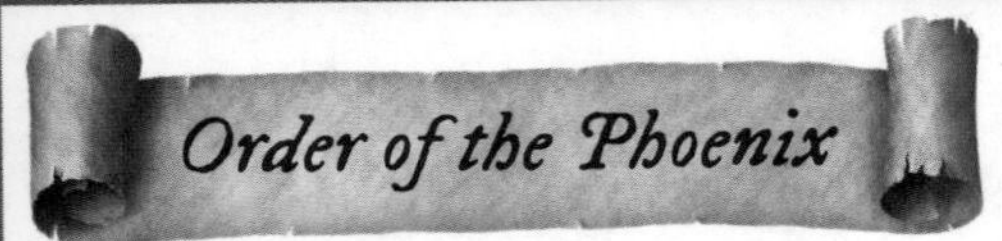

Your O.W.L. Exams: Year 5

Use your comprehensive knowledge from the past five years at Hogwarts to see if you can master this expert-level grab bag of wizarding knowledge.

13. Describe each DA member's Patronus (one point per answer):
Harry Potter ___________
Ron Weasley ___________
Hermione Granger ___________
Ginny Weasley ___________
Cho Chang ___________
Luna Lovegood ___________
Seamus Finnigan ___________
Ernie Macmillan ___________

14. List the incantation for all three Unforgivable Curses (one point each):
The Killing Curse ___________
The Imperius Curse ___________
The Cruciatus Curse ___________

15. Which of the following is NOT a defensive spell?
A. *Stupefy*
B. *Impedimenta*
C. *Expecto Patronum*
D. *Incendio*

16. Which of the following is the incantation for the Shield Charm?
A. *Protego*
B. *Protecto*
C. *Portus*
D. *Petrificus Totalus*

17. Professor Trelawney's great-great-grandmother was a famous Seer. What was her name?
A. Caroline
B. Cassie
C. Cassandra
D. Carolyn

18. How many legitimate prophecies has Professor Trelawney made (that we know of)?
A. 3
B. 2
C. 1
D. 5

COLLECTION CHRISTOPHEL/ALAMY

Bonnie Wright as Ginny Weasley and Oliver and James Phelps as her brothers Fred and George in *Harry Potter and the Order of the Phoenix* (2007).

Your O.W.L. Exams: Year 5

Use your comprehensive knowledge from the past five years at Hogwarts to see if you can master this expert-level grab bag of wizarding knowledge.

19. Complete the prophecy (one point per answer): "Neither can ____________ while the other ______."

20. Which of the following studies of Divination was NOT taught in Trelawney's class?
A. Dream interpretations
B. Crystal ball reading
C. Tea leaf reading
D. Bone reading

21. Which room in the Department of Mysteries contains all records of prophecies made?
A. The Hall of Prophecies
B. The Future Foyer
C. The Department of the Divine
D. The Room of Prophecies

22. Who replaced Trelawney after she was fired by Umbridge during Harry's fifth year?
A. Bane
B. Firenze
C. Ronan
D. Magorian

23. Can you put these events in the proper order?
___ Padfoot has his last laugh.
___ Order of the Phoenix members rescue Harry from the Dursleys and take him to Sirius's childhood home.
___ Mr. Weasley is attacked by Voldemort's snake while on Order of the Phoenix duty.
___ Harry receives his first detention from Umbridge and learns the cost of telling "lies."
___ Hagrid shows Harry and Hermione what he's been hiding in the Forbidden Forest.
___ Harry has his hearing at the Ministry of Magic for using magic outside of Hogwarts.
___ Umbridge is appointed High Inquisitor.
___ Harry, Ron, Hermione, Ginny, Neville and Luna travel to the Department of Mysteries after Harry has a vision of Sirius being tortured by Voldemort there.
___ Dumbledore's Army holds its first meeting.
___ Azkaban experiences a mass breakout, which includes the escape of Bellatrix Lestrange.
___ Harry saves Dudley and himself from dementors.
___ Harry discovers what's been pulling the seemingly horseless carriages.

Daniel Radcliffe as Harry Potter and Imelda Staunton as Professor Umbridge in *Harry Potter and the Order of the Phoenix* (2007).

The Heads of Hogwarts

The *Harry Potter* saga and *wizardingworld.com* mention 10 headmasters and headmistresses of Hogwarts: Can you match their names with their descriptions?

Armando Dippet	Everard
Dexter Fortescue	Severus Snape
Minerva McGonagall	Albus Dumbledore
Eupraxia Mole	Dolores Umbridge
Phineas Nigellus Black	Dilys Derwent

1. ____________________

In 1741, she left St. Mungo's to serve as headmistress of Hogwarts until 1768. Upon learning Arthur is injured, Headmaster Albus Dumbledore asks her to go between the headmaster's office and her other portrait at St. Mungo's.

2. ____________________

In his portrait, this headmaster can be found speaking loudly and using the same ear trumpet he used in life. His descendant owned an ice cream store in Diagon Alley.

3. ____________________

Became famous for the deal she made with Hogwarts poltergeist Peeves in 1876, as a result of which he agreed to stop causing havoc in exchange for a once-weekly swim in the boys' toilets, stale bread from the kitchen to throw and a custom-made hat from Madame Bonhabille (a French witch and hat-maker based in Paris).

Michael Gambon as Albus Dumbledore in *Harry Potter and the Order of the Phoenix* (2007).

4. ____________________

This headmaster uses his multiple portraits to warn Minerva McGonagall that Rufus Scrimgeour is on his way to Hogwarts from the Ministry of Magic after Dumbledore's death.

5. ____________________

This headmaster has a portrait hanging in the Order of the Phoenix's headquarters at 12 Grimmauld Place.

6. ____________________

During his time as headmaster, the Chamber of Secrets—created by Hogwarts founder Salazar Slytherin—is opened by Tom Riddle, unleashing the Basilisk within.

7. ____________________

She serves as headmistress of Hogwarts for a short period of time in 1996 after exposing Dumbledore's Army and being appointed by the Ministry through Educational Decree Number 28.

8. ____________________

This headmaster witnessed Sybill Trelawney, who had been hoping to be hired as a Divination professor at Hogwarts, make a prophecy about the birth of a child who would defeat the Dark Lord.

9. ____________________

During his tenure, Death Eaters Alecto and Amycus Carrow are appointed deputy heads.

10. ____________________

Following the Battle of Hogwarts, she undertakes the task of rebuilding the school and ensuring every student who was denied access by the Death Eaters is allowed to resume their studies.

FOR BONUS HOUSE POINTS

The Exploding Snap Test

Exploding Snap is a simple game of spotting pairs with the added twist of magical incendiary devices—this version tests your logic with explosive results!

AFTER BEING bamboozled by the wizard chess puzzles, Gryffindor's smartest student has devised a way to get revenge: bewitching an Exploding Snap deck to arrange itself into patterned sequences of nine cards, eight faceup and one facedown. If you can follow the patterned rows and guess the hidden cards, you win! If not, the cards will self-destruct!

Emma Watson as Hermione Granger.

FROM LEFT: PICTURELUX/THE HOLLYWOOD ARCHIVE/ALAMY; SHUTTERSTOCK (10)

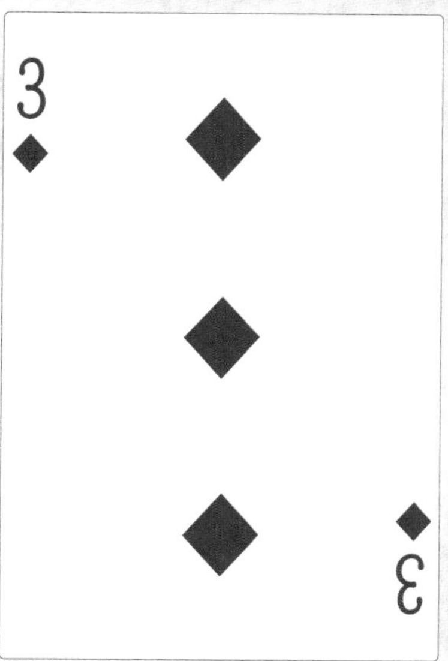

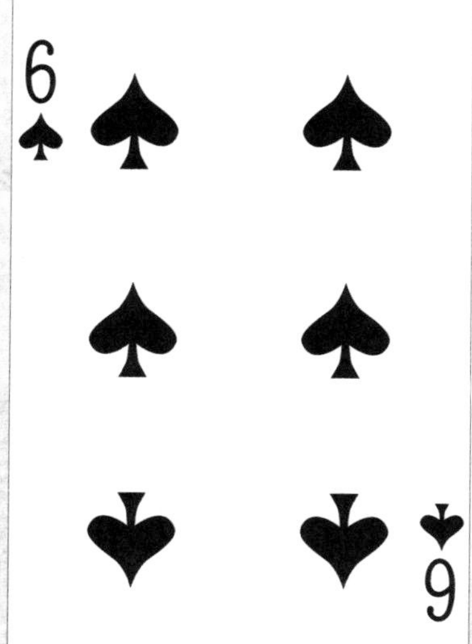

Teacher of the Year

1. What was Umbridge's job before becoming a professor at Hogwarts?
A. Senior Undersecretary to the Minister for Magic
B. Head of the Muggle-Born Registration Commission
C. Senior Undersecretary to the Head of Magical Law Enforcement
D. Head of the Office for the Detection and Confiscation of Counterfeit Defensive Spells and Protective Objects

2. How many Educational Decrees did the Ministry issue in total during Umbridge's tenure at Hogwarts?
A. 100
B. 28
C. 40
D. 36

3. Which Hogwarts House was Umbridge in while a student?

____

4. Name all the students Umbridge appointed to the Inquisitorial Squad mentioned by name:
(1) ____________________
(2) ____________________
(3) ____________________
(4) ____________________
(5) ____________________
(6) ____________________
(7) ____________________

5. What is the title of the book Umbridge assigned to her Defense Against the Dark Arts class?
A. *Applied Defensive Magic*
B. *Theoretical Defensive Magic*
C. *Defensive Magical Theory*
D. *Defensive Magical Education*

Professor Umbridge

Imelda Staunton as Professor Umbridge in *Harry Potter and the Order of the Phoenix* (2007).

Decrees of Separation

Can you tell the difference between Umbridge's real educational decrees and the faux? Use the space provided to reveal the ones that aren't telling lies.

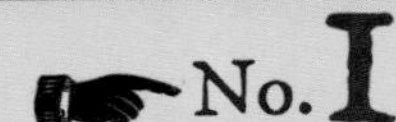
No. 1

In the event of the current headmaster being unable to provide a candidate for a teaching post, the Ministry should select an appropriate person.

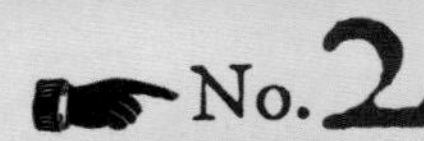
No. 2

The Inquisitorial Squad may award and remove House points in any manner they see fit.

No. 3

The High Inquisitor may administer Veritaserum whenever she sees fit in order to maintain order and uphold the rules at Hogwarts.

No. 4

No student organization, society, team, group or club may exist without the knowledge and approval of the High Inquisitor.

Did You Know?

The phone number Arthur Weasley dials on the keypad to enter the Ministry of Magic, 62442, spells "magic."

No. 5

Teachers are hereby banned from giving students any information that is not strictly related to the subjects they are paid to teach.

No. 6

No student may travel to Hogsmeade without the approval of the High Inquisitor.

No. 7

Any student found in possession of the magazine *The Quibbler* will be expelled.

No. 8

The High Inquisitor may oversee the grading practices of any subject taught at Hogwarts and adjust these practices when required.

No. 9

Dolores Jane Umbridge (High Inquisitor) has replaced Albus Dumbledore as Head of Hogwarts School of Witchcraft and Wizardry.

No. 10

Any student promoting rumors, lies and propaganda about He-Who-Must-Not-Be-Named's return will be expelled.

REAL DECREES:

____

____

Imelda Staunton as Dolores Umbridge in *Harry Potter and the Order of the Phoenix* (2007).

FOR BONUS HOUSE POINTS

Midnight Investigation

If donning the Invisibility Cloak and snooping on folks was a Hogwarts class, Harry would have been its star pupil. Can you use the following clues to figure out which of these characters he's following tonight?

1. If the person has a wand, they do not have a hat.
2. If the person is wearing a cloak, robe or dress, they are not wearing gloves.
3. If the person is a Slytherin, they do not have black hair.
4. If the person is a Ministry employee, they are not a member of the Order of the Phoenix.
5. If the person is a student, they do not have a wand.

Draco Malfoy

Cho Chang

Professor Snape

Professor Lockhart

Professor Flitwick

Professor Umbridge

(The Real) Mad-Eye Moody

The Ministry of Magic

Harry has had a vision of Arthur Weasley in grave danger at the Ministry of Magic. Can you help navigate the labyrinthine building to find him?

START

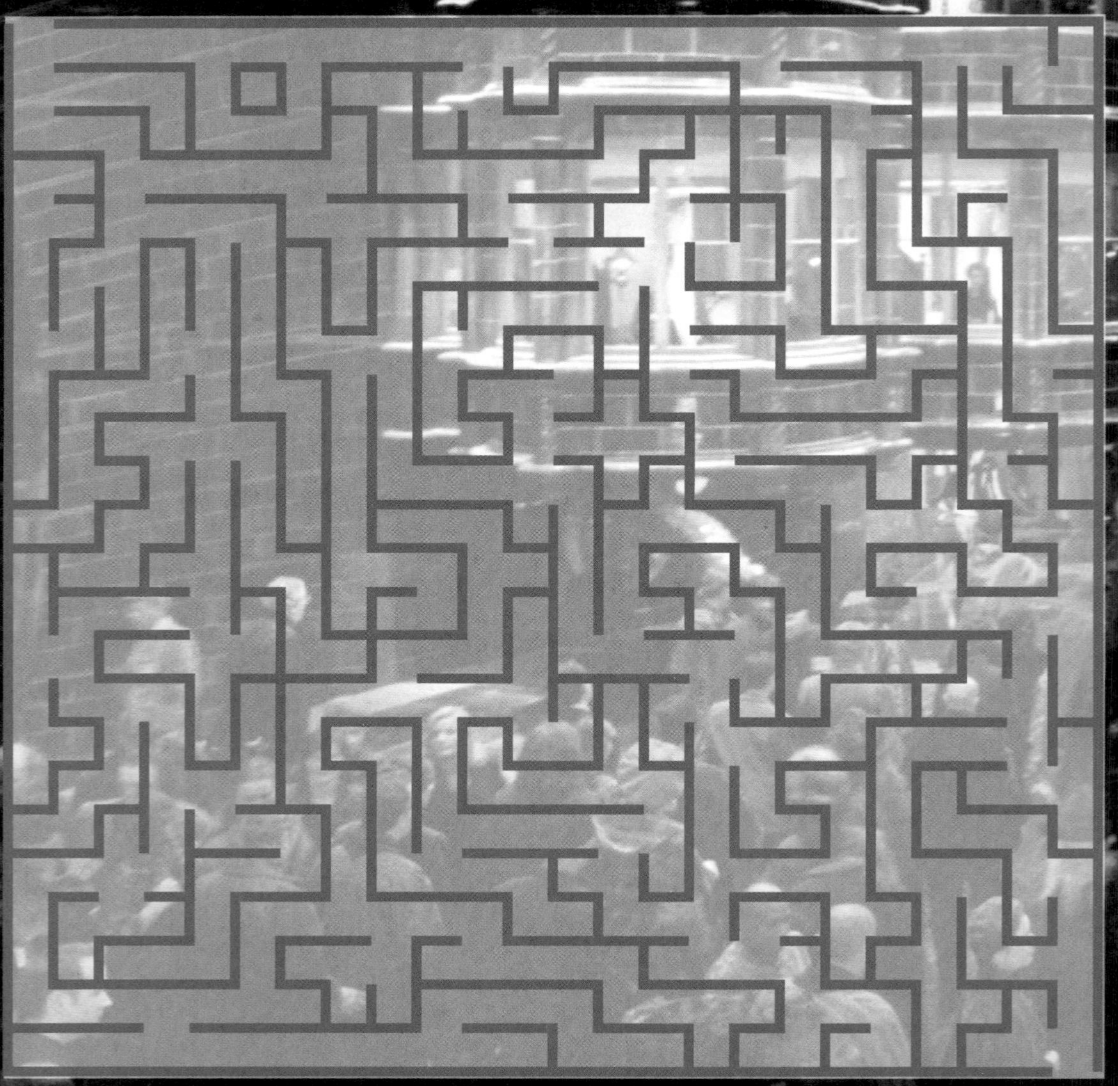

END

The entrance hall to the Ministry of Magic as seen in *Harry Potter and the Order of the Phoenix* (2007).

MuggleNet's Expert Trivia: Year 5

You must have been paying close attention to every word of the saga if you can answer all of these questions.

1. Which Care of Magical Creatures professor retired with only his arm and part of a leg intact?

____

2. Name the caretaker employed while Molly Weasley was in school.

____

3. In 1992, Mortlake was questioned about the experimental charming of what animals?

____

4. How many Gryffindor students signed the initial sign-up sheet in the Hog's Head to be a member of Dumbledore's Army?

____

Dumbledore's Army meets in the Room of Requirement in *Harry Potter and the Order of the Phoenix* (2007).

Harry Potter and the Half-Blood Prince

Dumbledore finally begins opening up to Harry during his sixth year, just before his tragic demise.

Daniel Radcliffe as Harry Potter and Michael Gambon as Albus Dumbledore in *Harry Potter and the Half-Blood Prince* (2009).

Did You Know?

The "tarnished tiara" Harry uses to mark the location of the Prince's copy of *Advanced Potion-Making* turns out to be Ravenclaw's diadem.

Fill-In-The-Blanks

After an epic duel between _______ _________ and ____________ at the Ministry, the wizarding world is finally convinced another __________ _____ is upon them. _______ _________ kidnap Ollivander and begin terrorizing both the wizarding and Muggle worlds. Meanwhile at Hogwarts, Professor __________ has come out of retirement to become the new Potions master, and ______ finally gets the Dark Arts job he's been pining after. In Potions, Harry is lucky enough to be given an old textbook with extremely helpful notes in the margins, provided by one who calls himself the ______-_____ ______. Harry and Dumbledore try to collect Voldemort's __________, and Harry and _______ finally get together. Finally, _____ _______ is given a dark task by Voldemort: Kill ______ __________. When Draco's nerve fails him, it is _______ who casts the fatal curse.

Daniel Radcliffe as Harry Potter in *Harry Potter and the Half-Blood Prince* (2009).

The Location Code

In the sixth installment of the *Harry Potter* saga, Harry sees more of the wizarding world beyond Hogwarts than ever before. Can you unscramble the locations pertinent to *Harry Potter and the Half-Blood Prince* with the help of the following clues?

When Harry arrives here in *Harry Potter and the Half-Blood Prince*, all the hands on the location's unique clock are pointed toward "mortal peril."

HET BRUWOR

____

Although a house on the outskirts of this village appears in *Harry Potter and the Goblet of Fire*, the town isn't described until the sixth installment of the saga.

TLIELT AHNLOTNEG

____

Harry inherits a property on this London thoroughfare at the beginning of the book.

GIRMAMLUD APLEC

____

At the beginning of the book, Snape meets with Narcissa Malfoy and Bellatrix Lestrange in a house on this street.

ISPNENR'S NED

____

In a callback to the first book, Harry and Draco meet in a Diagon Alley shop owned by this witch.

AMDAM ALMIKN

____

This store, owned by someone we later learn is imprisoned at Malfoy Manor, closes in the sixth installment.

LOLIVENADRS

____

Fred and George harbored plans to buy this Hogsmeade joke shop until Hogwarts students' trips to the village were canceled.

ONOKZ'S

____

When Narcissa Malfoy encounters Harry, Ron and Hermione shopping at a clothing store in Diagon Alley, she threatens to take her business to this other boutique.

WITLTIFT NAD TTATNIG'S

____

Did You Know?

The Elder Wand's core is a Thestral hair.

Hogwarts Curriculum: Year 6

How closely were you paying attention to the *Harry Potter* books and films?

1. The actor who plays a young Voldemort at the orphanage is related to Ralph Fiennes, who plays the adult iteration, in real life. How are they related?
A. Son
B. Nephew
C. Cousin

2. Which scene was added to the *Half-Blood Prince* movie that wasn't in the book?
A. The Death Eater battle at the Burrow
B. The Slug Club Christmas party
C. The Felix Felicis scene

3. *Half-Blood Prince* is the first movie to...
A. Show Voldemort as Tom Riddle
B. Show Harry spending Christmas somewhere other than Hogwarts
C. Not feature a Defense Against the Dark Arts class

4. While reading the script for *Half-Blood Prince*, J.K. Rowling had to correct a line because it incorrectly assumed...
A. Dumbledore was heterosexual
B. Bellatrix had no children
C. The Half-Blood Prince was evil

5. What was the movie's tagline?
A. Dark secrets revealed
B. The rebellion begins
C. Nowhere is safe

Hero Fiennes Tiffin as young Tom Riddle.

Jim Broadbent as Horace Slughorn and Daniel Radcliffe as Harry Potter in *Harry Potter and the Half-Blood Prince* (2009).

Hogwarts Curriculum: Year 6

How closely were you paying attention to the *Harry Potter* books and films?

6. How many girls did Jessie Cave best in the audition process to land the role of Lavender Brown?
A. 10,000
B. 8,000
C. 7,000

7. Professor Slughorn's office looks a little familiar. What room did Slughorn's office appear as in the fifth movie?
A. Dumbledore's Office
B. Room of Requirement
C. The Defense Against the Dark Arts classroom

8. Director David Yates based his lighting schemes and color palette on the paintings of which Dutch Master?

____

9. The spell ____________, used in *Harry Potter and the Half-Blood Prince*, is "for enemies."

10. ____________ can be used as an incantation to fill the ears of those around you with an uncontrollable buzzing.

11. When in need of an impromptu fire extinguisher, the spell ____________ will do the trick.

Emma Watson as Hermione Granger in *Harry Potter and the Half-Blood Prince* (2009).

Hogwarts Curriculum: Year 6

How closely were you paying attention to the *Harry Potter* books and films?

12. Apart from Peeves, the incantation Langlock is used by Harry on which other Hogwarts character? ______________

13. Snape saves Draco from a powerful dark spell with the countercurse ______________

14. Can you match the event to the chapter of *Half-Blood Prince* in which it occurred?

Event:

A. Romilda Vane tries to slip Harry a love potion.

B. Ron, Harry, Hermione and Ginny visit Fred and George's new shop.

C. Rufus Scrimgeour takes over for Cornelius Fudge.

D. Dumbledore and Harry arrive back at Hogwarts to find the Dark Mark.

E. Snape makes an Unbreakable Vow.

F. The Pensieve makes its first appearance in *Half-Blood Prince*.

G. Harry first says that Draco has become a Death Eater.

Chapter:

1. The Other Minister__
2. Spinner's End __
3. Draco's Detour __
4. The Slug Club __
5. The House of Gaunt __
6. The Unbreakable Vow__
7. The Lightning-Struck Tower __

Alfred Enoch as Dean Thomas, Emma Watson as Hermione Granger, Matthew Lewis as Neville Longbottom and Rupert Grint as Ron Weasley in *Harry Potter and the Half-Blood Prince* (2009).

Michael Gambon as Albus Dumbledore and Daniel Radcliffe as Harry Potter in *Harry Potter and the Half-Blood Prince* (2009).

Pensieve Lessons

What better way to learn from past experiences than to relive them as a fly on the wall? If only you had a Pensieve for this quiz.

1. Harry and Dumbledore's first trip into the Pensieve sees them visit the village of ______ _________ with Bob Ogden.

2. Ogden uses a ________ jinx to stop Marvolo Gaunt from harming his daughter.

3. What ability does Tom Riddle admit he has to Dumbledore before he leaves the orphanage?

____

4. Dumbledore reveals Voldemort used a memory modifying charm on his uncle Morfin during one of his collected memories. Who is the only other character confirmed to have used this spell?

____

5. What words did Professor Slughorn add to the end of his memory in which Riddle asks about Horcruxes, tampering with it to cover his tracks?

____ __ ______, ___, _____ __ ______

6. From whom does Voldemort acquire Slytherin's Locket and Hufflepuff's Cup?

________________ ________________

Michael Gambon as Albus Dumbledore in *Harry Potter and the Goblet of Fire* (2005). The Pensieve is introduced in this story.

FROM LEFT: JAAP BUITENDIJK/WARNER BROS/EVERETT COLLECTION; ALBUM/ALAMY

The Horcrux Chronicles

Can you remember the pertinent facts about the fate of each bit of Tom Riddle's soul?

Thinking that _________ was the safest place possible for his first experiment in Horcrux-making, Tom Riddle turned his _________ into a Horcrux. Though this artifact would eventually make its way into the hands of a wealthy private collector, it would be surreptitiously placed with the school books of first-year student _________ _________, setting a petrifying chain of events in motion.

Searching out items imbued with personal history, Voldemort finds a _______ belonging to his grandfather _______ _______ and turns it into a Horcrux. Unbeknownst to him, however, this item is also a _______ _______.

When Voldemort went searching for relics of the Hogwarts founders to turn into Horcruxes, he found two at once: a ____ belonging to Helga _________ and a locket belonging to ________ _________, the founder of Tom Riddle's Hogwarts House.

Using his charm on the ghost of ________ Tower, ___ ________ _________, Voldemort is able to convince her to lead him to a ________ belonging to another Hogwarts founder. He then turns this into a Horcrux that is eventually destroyed by Death Eater incompetence.

Voldemort also created two Horcruxes out of ________ creatures. The first was his snake, _______, who was transformed into a Horcrux thanks to the killing of _______ _______. Voldemort is unaware of having created the second, but he did so on the night of October 31, 1981: _______ _______.

Did You Know?

Harry sees Mundungus Fletcher and Aberforth Dumbledore speaking before he confronts Mundungus about stealing from No. 12, Grimmauld Place. In *Deathly Hallows*, it is revealed that Mundungus sold Aberforth Sirius's mirror during this interaction, the mirror that helped Aberforth connect with Harry throughout his Horcrux hunt.

Coded Common Room Passwords

Can you break the codes and provide a forgetful student with the next six passwords to Gryffindor common room?

GRYFFINDOR'S MOST forgetful student has had to sleep out in the hallway once or twice because the password slipped his mind. So he's been provided with a list of the passwords to Gryffindor Tower for the next six weeks. But just in case they fall into the wrong hands, the passwords have been encoded. The only problem is that one hapless Gryffindor is having trouble cracking the codes. Can you help?

Rupert Grint as Ron Weasley in
Harry Potter and the Half-Blood Prince (2009).

1. KMXST JVMKYZEU

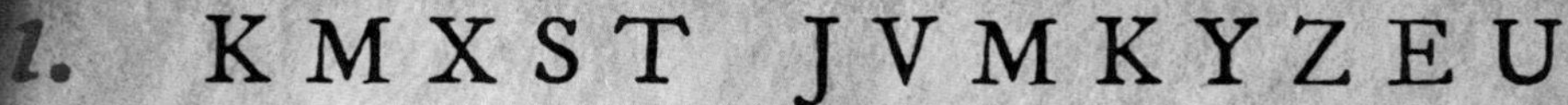

Hint: In Sorcerer's Stone, *Percy Weasley is the first person Harry hears use this password.*

2. ULUS BNIM MOAI ITXM MELB

Hint: This password is an herbological reference to a type of cactus.

3. NAMA UROJ TROF

Hint: This Latin-derived password translates to "greater fortune."

4. TOWIB ZWUVGH

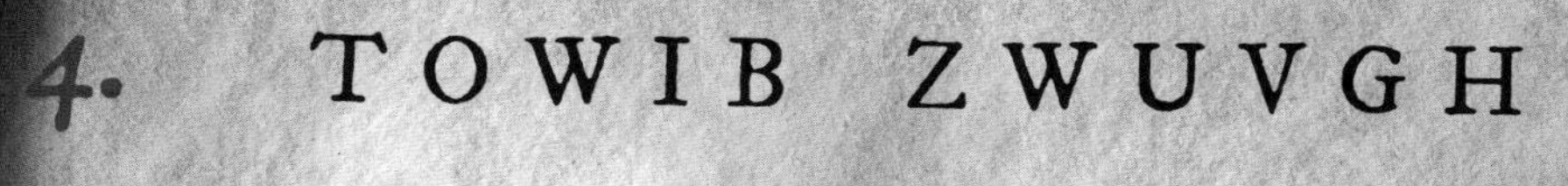

Hint: This password appears in Chapter 22 of Goblet of Fire.

5. SKOD NIBD IDSO

Hint: This password is used in the same chapter in which Harry begins his Patronus lessons with Professor Lupin.

6. SH AD ER DL BA

Hint: This password is also the name of a popular Muggle board game.

FOR BONUS HOUSE POINTS

The Lions of Gryffindor

It might take some brain racking to remember the names of every player to compete for Gryffindor during Harry's time at Hogwarts. Can you name them in the spaces opposite?

NAME:	YEARS:
1.	1-3, 5
2.	5
3.	1-3, 5
4.	6
5.	6
6.	6
7.	1-3, 5
8.	1-3, 5
9.	5-6
10.	6
11.	5
12.	1-3, 5-6
13.	1-3
14.	5-6
15.	6

MuggleNet's Expert Trivia: Year 6

You must have been paying close attention to every word of the saga if you can answer all of these questions.

1. Which educational decree number makes Dolores Umbridge the new Head of Hogwarts?

____

2. In the Hufflepuff Common room, what is Helga Hufflepuff's portrait doing?

____

3. What is Professor Grubbly-Plank's first name?

____

4. What food did Dumbledore enjoy with Lupin when inviting him to study at Hogwarts?

____

Richard Leaf as John Dawlish, Imelda Staunton as Dolores Umbridge, Robert Hardy as Cornelius Fudge and George Harris as Kinglsey Shacklebolt in *Harry Potter and the Order of the Phoenix* (2007). After her role as Headmistress of Hogwarts, Umbridge returns to the Ministry.

The Noble and Most Ancient House of Black

Their motto is "Toujours Pur," and they won't let anyone forget it. Can you fill in the Black family tree?

Daniel Radcliffe as Harry Potter and Gary Oldman as Sirius Black in front of the Black family tree at 12 Grimmauld Place.

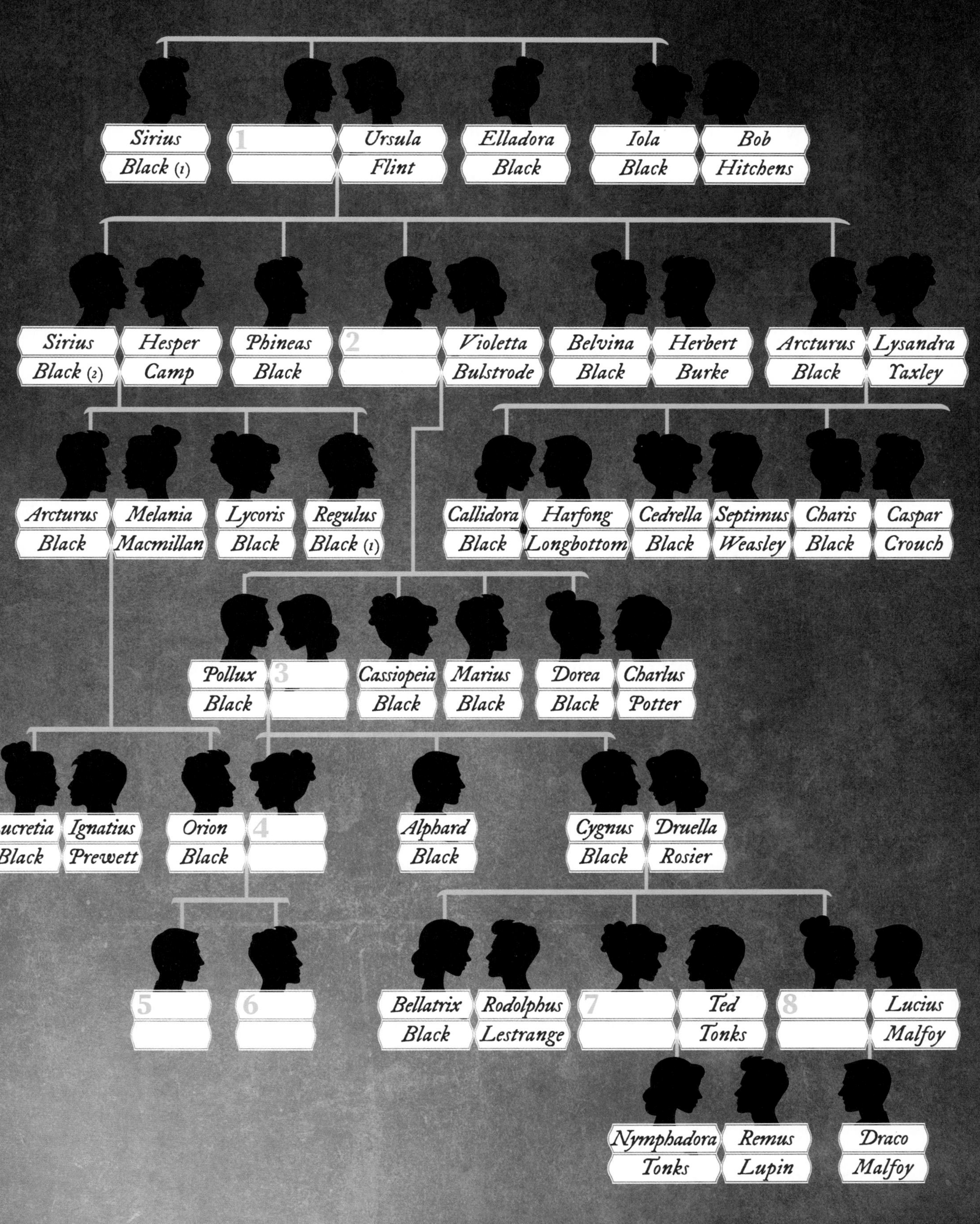

Sirius Black (1)
1
Ursula Flint
Elladora Black
Iola Black
Bob Hitchens
Sirius Black (2)
Hesper Camp
Phineas Black
2
Violetta Bulstrode
Belvina Black
Herbert Burke
Arcturus Black
Lysandra Yaxley
Arcturus Black
Melania Macmillan
Lycoris Black
Regulus Black (1)
Callidora Black
Harfong Longbottom
Cedrella Black
Septimus Weasley
Charis Black
Caspar Crouch
Pollux Black
3
Cassiopeia Black
Marius Black
Dorea Black
Charlus Potter
Lucretia Black
Ignatius Prewett
Orion Black
4
Alphard Black
Cygnus Black
Druella Rosier
5
6
Bellatrix Black
Rodolphus Lestrange
7
Ted Tonks
8
Lucius Malfoy
Nymphadora Tonks
Remus Lupin
Draco Malfoy

The Half-Blood Prince's Textbook

Can you remember these expert-level bits of trivia from the story of Harry and Snape and unlock the Half-Blood Prince's secret side notes?

1. In the chapter "Birthday Surprises," Harry is disappointed to find that the "Prince" had made no notes on:
   A. Golpalott's Third Law
   B. Gamp's Fifth Law
   C. Dagworth's Second Law
   D. Galician's Fourth Law

2. What is the counter-jinx to *Levicorpus*?
   A. *Levicorpus*
   B. *Descecorpus*
   C. *Liberacorpus*
   D. *Tombecorpus*

3. Who invented the incantation *Langlock*?
   A. Albus Dumbledore
   B. Newt Scamander
   C. James Potter
   D. Severus Snape

4. On the day of Hermione's Apparition test, Harry makes the Prince's heavily corrected version of which potion?
   A. Hiccoughing Solution
   B. Cheering Draught
   C. Draught of Peace
   D. Elixir to Induce Euphoria

5. When finished, what shade of yellow is the Elixir to Induce Euphoria?
   A. Mustard
   B. Sunshine
   C. Butter
   D. Daffodil

6. Harry hides *Advanced Potion-Making* in a cupboard in the Room of Requirement,

next to a skeleton with how many legs?

A. 1
B. 3
C. 5
D. 7

7. According to Snape's notes, the incantation *Sectumsempra* should be used against whom?

A. Muggles
B. Werewolves
C. Enemies
D. James Potter

8. According to Slughorn, which ingredient counterbalances the side effects of the Elixir to Induce Euphoria?

A. Cheese
B. Boomslang skin
C. Peppermint
D. Honey

9. What was Snape's self-given moniker the "Half-Blood Prince" inspired by?

A. His godfather
B. His favorite teacher
C. A famous potioneer
D. His mother's maiden name

10. Harry used the incantation *Levicorpus* on which one of his friends?

A. Ron
B. Neville
C. Luna
D. Hermione

Alan Rickman as Severus Snape in *Harry Potter and the Half-Blood Prince* (2009).

Harry Potter and the Deathly Hallows (and Beyond)

Instead of studying for his N.E.W.T.s by the common room fire, Harry spends what should be his final year at Hogwarts hunting Horcruxes.

Daniel Radcliffe as Harry Potter, Rupert Grint as Ron Weasley and Emma Watson as Hermione Granger in *Harry Potter and the Deathly Hallows: Part 2* (2011).

Did You Know?

Professor Trelawney states in *Prisoner of Azkaban* that when 13 dine together, the first to rise is the first to die. When 13 people share a bottle of firewhisky after the Battle of the Seven Potters, Lupin is the first to leave and, eventually, the first of the group to die.

Fill-In-The-Blanks

Still reeling from the death of Dumbledore, Harry and his best friends decide to drop out of ________ to complete the search for Voldemort's __________. While they celebrate the wedding of ________ _________ and _______ __________, the ___________ ___ ________ falls to the Death Eaters and Harry, Ron and Hermione are forced to make a hasty getaway. They begin living life on the run as they continue their search, but the stress leads to a fracture in the group when ______ leaves, returning just in time to help Harry destroy the _______ of ________. Eventually, their journey takes them back to Hogwarts, now under Death Eater control, where they find that __________ ______ has been waging a guerrilla war against the new headmaster, _______. Harry's presence at Hogwarts brings both the Order of the Phoenix and the Death Eaters to Hogwarts for a final battle, in which Harry sacrifices himself, destroying the Horcrux within. After Harry returns from the brink of death, _____ __________ kills Voldemort's snake, _____, the final Horcrux, allowing Voldemort to be defeated once and for all.

Daniel Radcliffe as Harry Potter leading his cohorts into the Lestrange vault at Gringotts in *Harry Potter and the Deathly Hallows: Part 2* (2011).

Daniel Radcliffe as the "Seven Potters," members of the Order of the Phoenix transformed by Polyjuice Potion, in *Harry Potter and the Deathly Hallows: Part 1* (2010).

The Seven Potters

We give you the mode of transport and the bodyguard—can you remember the Harry Potter decoy?

1. Thestral, with Kingsley Shacklebolt ______________

2. Broomstick, with Arthur Weasley ________________

3. Thestral, with Bill Weasley _______________

4. Broomstick, with Mad-Eye Moody ___________

5. Motorbike, with Hagrid _______________

6. Broomstick, with Tonks _________________

7. Broomstick, with Lupin _________________

Robbie Coltrane as Rubeus Hagrid and Daniel Radcliffe as *Harry Potter in Harry Potter and the Deathly Hallows: Part I* (2010).

Dumbledore's Will

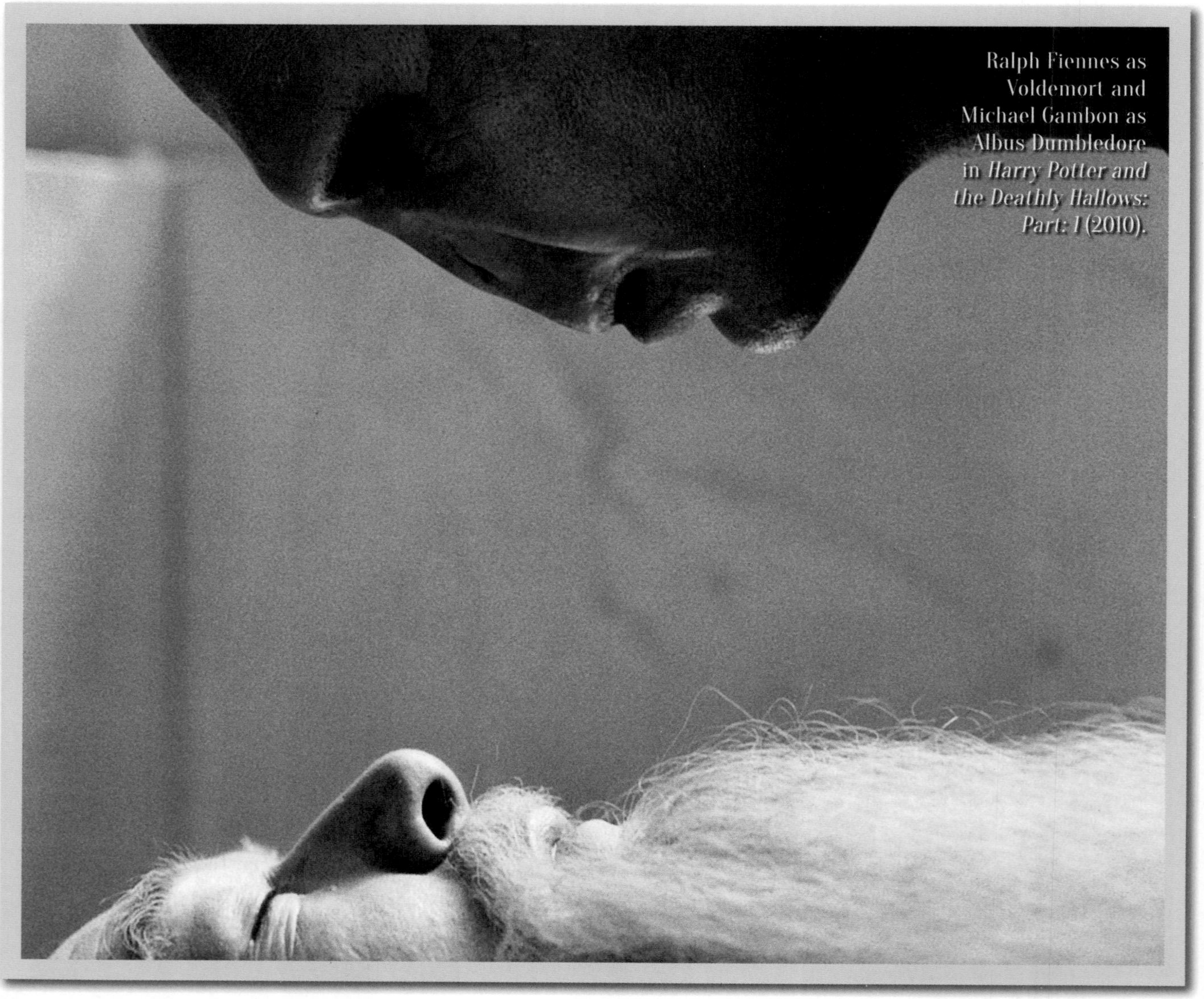

Ralph Fiennes as Voldemort and Michael Gambon as Albus Dumbledore in *Harry Potter and the Deathly Hallows: Part 1* (2010).

FROM LEFT: PICTURELUX/THE HOLLYWOOD ARCHIVE/ALAMY; SHUTTERSTOCK

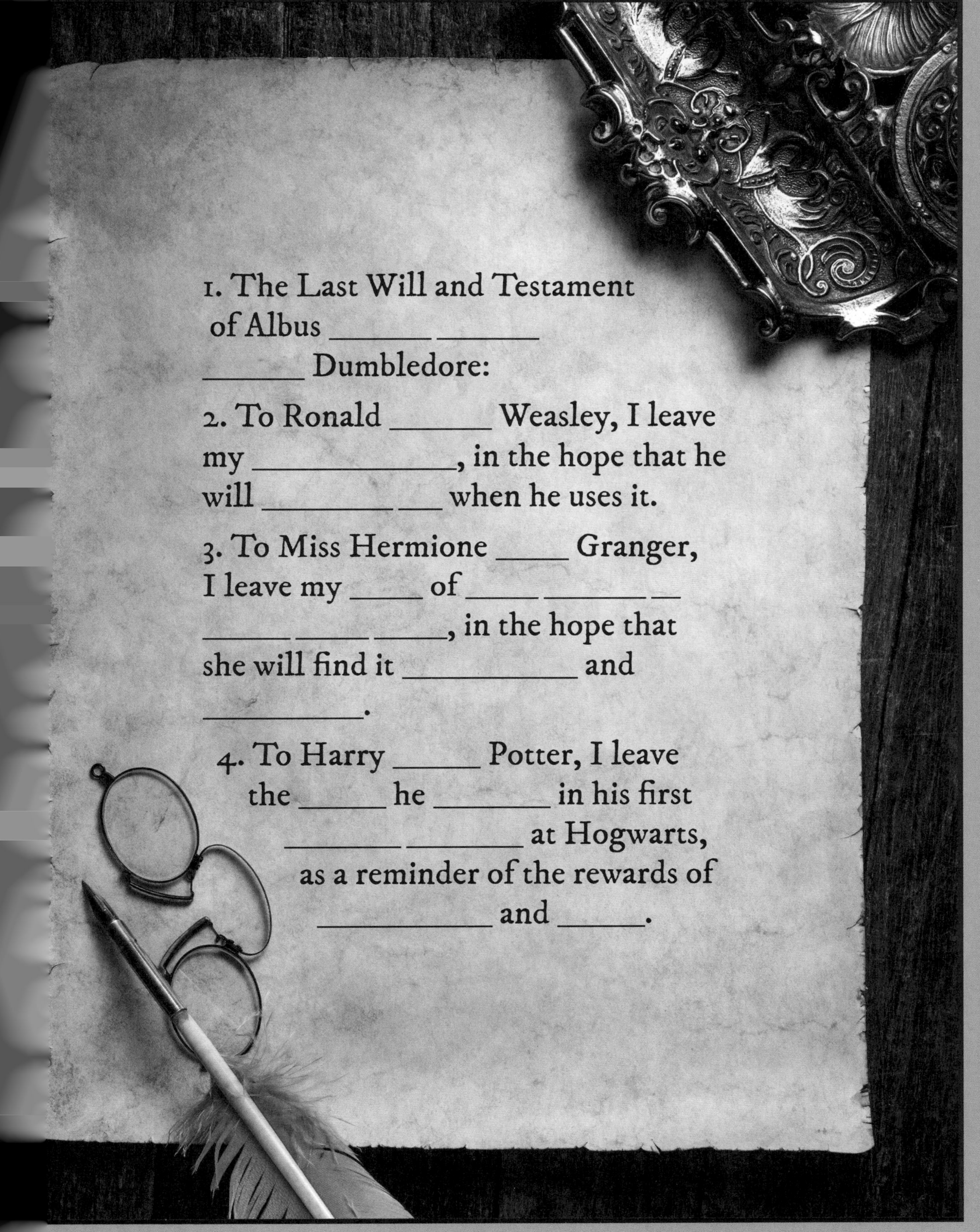
1. The Last Will and Testament of Albus ______ ______ ______ Dumbledore:

2. To Ronald ______ Weasley, I leave my ____________, in the hope that he will ________ ___ when he uses it.

3. To Miss Hermione _____ Granger, I leave my _____ of _____ ______ __ _____ _____ _____, in the hope that she will find it __________ and __________.

4. To Harry _____ Potter, I leave the _____ he _______ in his first _______ _______ at Hogwarts, as a reminder of the rewards of ___________ and _____.

N.E.W.T. Exams: Year 7

Use your comprehensive knowledge from the past seven years at Hogwarts to see if you can master this expert-level grab bag of wizarding knowledge.

1. What is the only one of the Five Principal Exceptions to Gamp's Law of Elemental Transfiguration mentioned explicitly in the *Harry Potter* series? ___________________

2. In J.K. Rowling's original notes, the subject of Transfiguration was rendered as Transfiguration/___________________.

3. Where do vanished objects go?___________

4. The first recorded Animagus in wizarding history was Falco Aesalon, a wizard from which country?

____

5. What is the incantation for the Charm Harry casts between Molly Weasley and Voldemort during the Battle of Hogwarts?

____

Ralph Fiennes as Voldemort in *Harry Potter and the Deathly Hallows: Part 2* (2011).

Daniel Radcliffe as Harry Potter in *Harry Potter and the Deathly Hallows: Part 1* (2010).

N.E.W.T. Exams: Year 7

Use your comprehensive knowledge from the past seven years at Hogwarts to see if you can master this expert-level grab bag of wizarding knowledge.

6. *Capacious extremis* is the incantation for which charm, used by Hermione in *Harry Potter and the Deathly Hallows*?

____

7. *Anapneo* is a spell used by which Hogwarts professor to allow a student to breathe?

____

8. This incantation can be used to stop a falling object.

____

9. A Caterwauling Charm is used by Death Eaters near which wizarding location to catch people out after curfew? ____________________

10. What is the incantation for the Blasting Curse, used by Hermione in an attempt to kill Nagini?

____

Daniel Radcliffe as Harry Potter in *Harry Potter and the Deathly Hallows: Part 1* (2010).

Rupert Grint as Ron Weasley, Emma Watson as Hermione Granger and Daniel Radcliffe as Harry Potter in *Harry Potter and the Deathly Hallows: Part 2* (2011).

N.E.W.T. Exams: Year 7

Use your comprehensive knowledge from the past seven years at Hogwarts to see if you can master this expert-level grab bag of wizarding knowledge.

11. Which spell is used by Harry to carve Dobby's epitaph?

____

12. This healing essence used in *Harry Potter and the Deathly Hallows* is based on a real herbal anti-inflammatory.

____

13. The use of this potion is described by Horace Slughorn as illegal in competitions.

____

14. During preparation for N.E.W.T.s in their sixth year, Harry and Hermione study these potions, which can magically refill themselves indefinitely.

____

15. Who wrote *Advanced Potion-Making*? ________________

Daniel Radcliffe as Harry Potter and Ralph Fiennes as Voldemort in *Harry Potter and the Deathly Hallows: Part 1* (2010).

Josh Herdman as Gregory Goyle and Tom Felton as Draco Malfoy in *Harry Potter and the Deathly Hallows: Part 2* (2011).

N.E.W.T. Exams: Year 7

Use your comprehensive knowledge from the past seven years at Hogwarts to see if you can master this expert-level grab bag of wizarding knowledge.

16. This spell is used by Hermione and Harry to repel hexes from their temporary campsites in *Harry Potter and the Deathly Hallows*.

____

17. This curse was used by Mad-Eye to protect 12 Grimmauld Place against Snape. _______________

18. Which spell does Lupin fear will give Harry away to the Death Eaters? _______________

19. Who is the first member of the Order of the Phoenix to kill a witch or wizard with *Avada Kedavra* in the series? _______________

20. How many galleons did the reward for the capture of Harry Potter reach at its peak?

____

Mark Williams as Arthur Weasley and Bonnie Wright as Ginny Weasley in *Harry Potter and the Deathly Hallows: Part 2* (2011).

Daniel Radcliffe as Harry Potter, Rupert Grint as Ron Weasley and Emma Watson as Hermione Granger in *Harry Potter and the Deathly Hallows: Part 1* (2010).

Escape From Malfoy Manor

During the Second Wizarding War, the Malfoys kept a private prison at the behest of Lord Voldemort. Can you escape before the Dark Lord arrives?

Jason Isaacs as Lucius Malfoy, Helen McCrory as Narcissa Malfoy and Tom Felton as Draco Malfoy in *Harry Potter and the Deathly Hallows: Part 1* (2010).

Clockwise from top: Helena Bonham Carter as Bellatrix Lestrange in *Harry Potter and the Deathly Hallows: Part 2* (2011); Emma Watson as Hermione Granger, Dave Legeno as Fenrir Greyback and Rupert Grint as Ron Weasley in *Harry Potter and the Deathly Hallows: Part 2* (2011); Dobby (voiced by Toby Jones) in *Harry Potter and the Deathly Hallows: Part 1* (2010).

Deathly Hallows

Emma Watson as Hermione Granger, Rupert Grint as Ron Weasley, Daniel Radcliffe as Harry Potter and Rhys Ifans as Xenophilius Lovegood in *Harry Potter and the Deathly Hallows: Part 1* (2010).

The Tale of the Three Brothers

This wizarding fairy tale is the key to understanding the Deathly Hallows. How well do you know it?

1. "The Tale of the Three Brothers" can be found in *The Tales of* _____ ____ ______.

2. When Hermione reads it aloud, Ron interrupts, taking issue with the setting. His mother always said the brothers were walking at _______, rather than ________.

3. The three brothers cheated Death by magically creating a ______, so they could cross a ________.

4. Death gifted the first brother with the most _____ _____ in existence. It has to ____ duels for its owner.

5. The second brother requested a means of recalling loved ones from the dead. He was given the ___________ Stone.

6. More humble than his other brothers, the third brother asked for a way to ____ Death. Death gave the brother his ____ __ _______.

7. The first brother was murdered and had his wand stolen ___ days after receiving it.

8. After turning the Stone ___ times in his hand, the second brother was reunited with his deceased lover, but there was a ______ between them. In despair, he killed himself.

9. Years later, the third brother ____ Death like an _____ __________ and gave the Cloak to _____ _____.

A True Gryffind

Matthew Lewis as Neville Longbottom in *Harry Potter and the Deathly Hallows: Part 2* (2011).

RGR COLLECTION/ALAMY (2)

or

Neville's big moment came at the Battle of Hogwarts. Can you spot the six differences in this pivotal scene?

Deathly Hallows

The United Kingdom of Magic

Can you fill in the magical locations on this map of Britain with the help of the clues provided?

1. A running start will get you onto this secret loading dock in Britain's capital.
2. This wizarding district was filmed at the vast Leadenhall Market in London.
3. The only all-wizard town in Britain.
4. The alma mater of Britain's finest wizards.
5. Hermione's parents once took her on a camping trip to this location in England, where she later hides out with Harry and Ron.
6. The Midlands village in which Severus Snape and Lily Evans grew up.
7. The location where the Minister of Magic visits his Muggle counterpart.
8. The suburban town in which 4 Privet Drive can be found.
9. Harry's ancestral village.
10. The town in which one might find the Burrow.

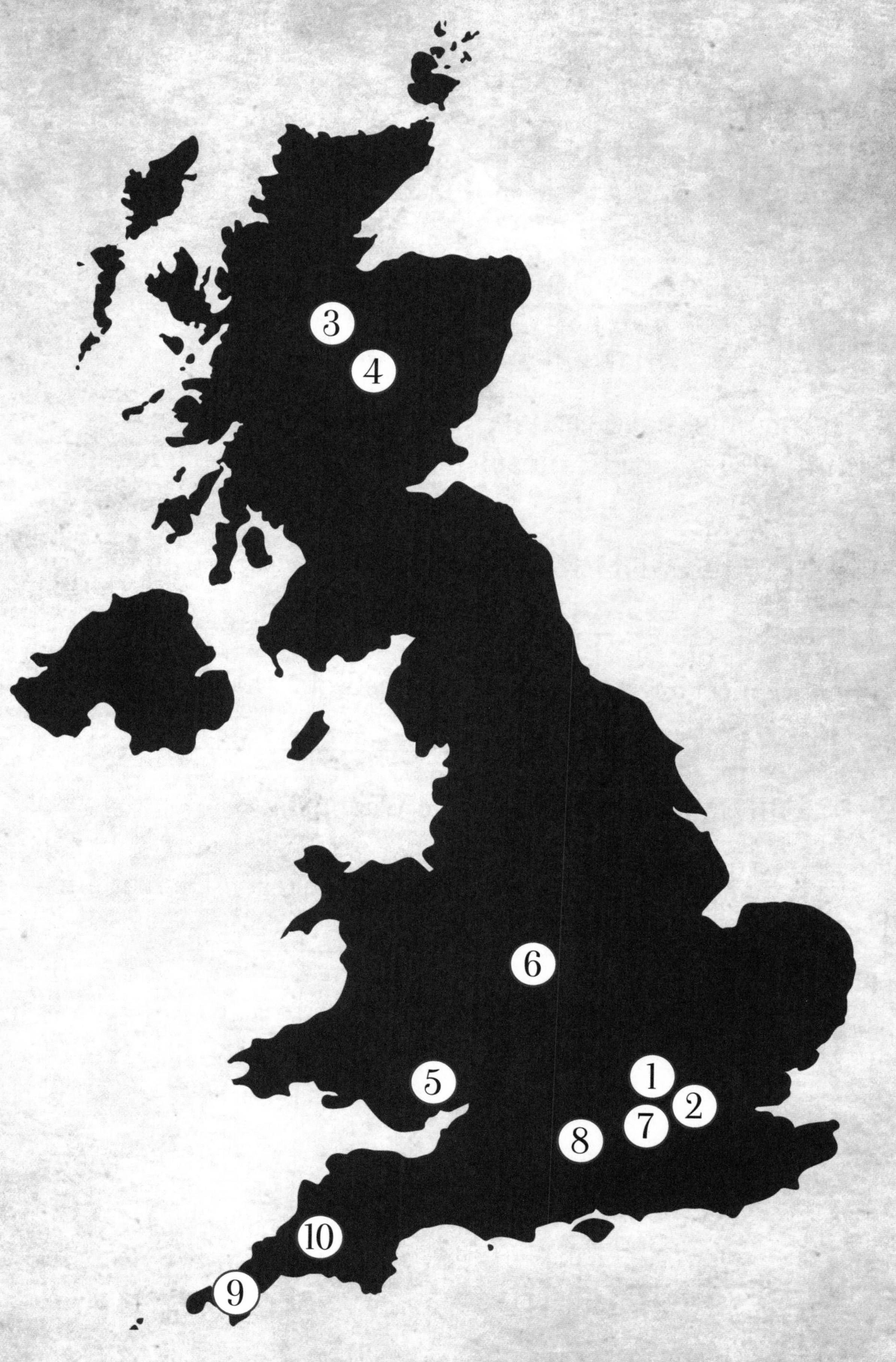

SHUTTERSTOCK (2)

MuggleNet's Expert Trivia: Year 7

You must have been paying close attention to every word of the saga if you can answer all of these questions.

1. Which creatures did Elphias Doge narrowly escape on his world tour?

   ____

2. When we meet a wizard known only as Bob, what animal is he holding?

   ____

3. Ollivanders: Makers of Fine Wands since ________ B.C.

4. In which classroom does Firenze teach Divination?

   ____

Rupert Grint as Ron Weasley and Daniel Radcliffe as Harry Potter in *Harry Potter and the Deathly Hallows: Part 2* (2011).

Worldwide Wizarding

Can you decipher the book, country of origin and language for each of these J.K. Rowling titles?

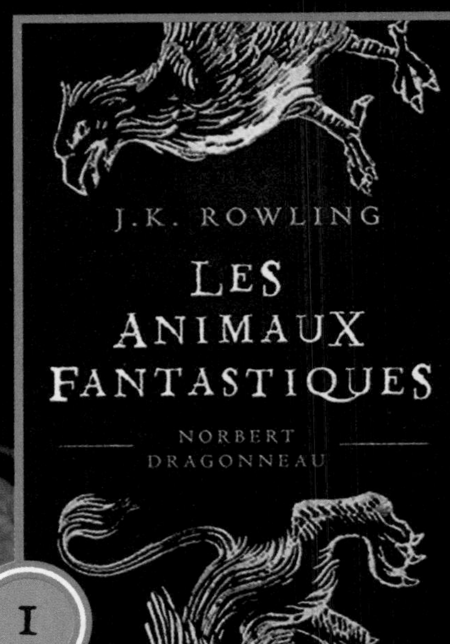

1

Title ______________________
Country ______________________
Language ______________________

5

Title ______________________
Country ______________________
Language ______________________

6

Title ______________________
Country ______________________
Language ______________________

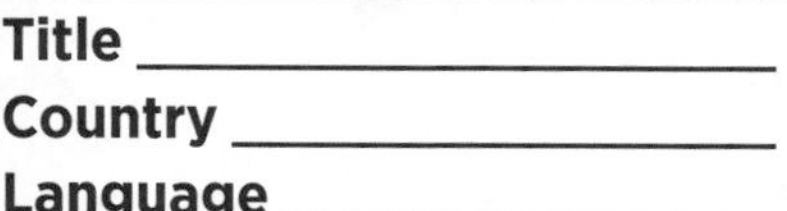
Title ____________________
Country __________________
Language ________________

Title ____________________
Country __________________
Language ________________

Title ____________________
Country __________________
Language ________________

Title ____________________
Country __________________
Language ________________

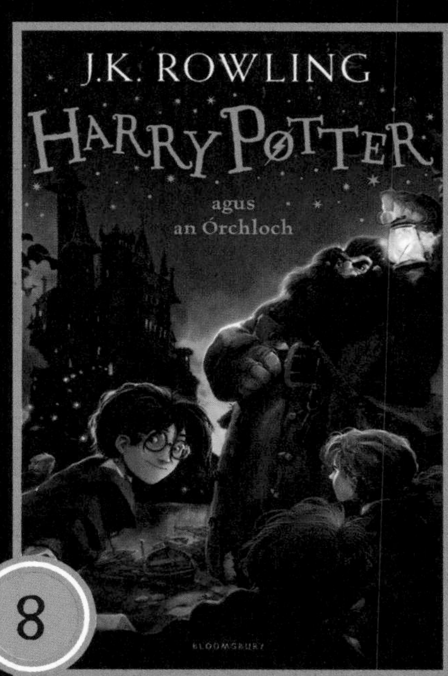

Title ____________________
Country __________________
Language ________________

Title ____________________
Country __________________
Language ________________

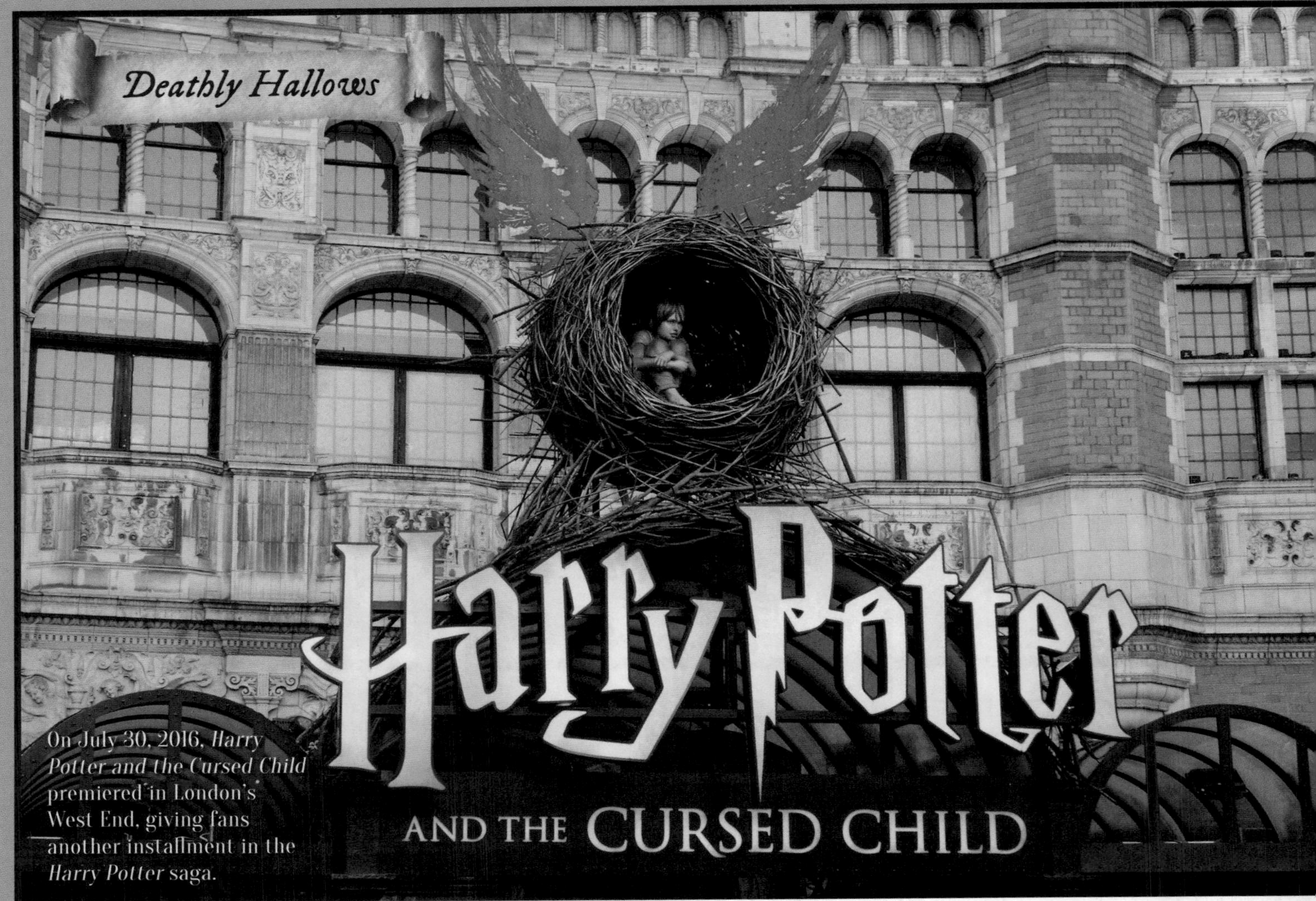

On July 30, 2016, *Harry Potter and the Cursed Child* premiered in London's West End, giving fans another installment in the *Harry Potter* saga.

Cursed Catch-Up

Nineteen years after the Battle of Hogwarts, where are our favorite characters at the start of *Cursed Child*?

1. Of which Ministry of Magic Department is Harry the head?
A. Magical Law Enforcement
B. International Magical Cooperations
C. Magical Games and Sports
D. Magical Transportation

2. Who is the Minister of Magic at the start of *Cursed Child*?
A. Kingsley Shacklebolt
B. Hermione Granger
C. Draco Malfoy
D. Dedalus Diggle

3. What is Ron's job title 19 years later?
A. Head of the Auror Office
B. Head of Misuse of Muggle Artifacts
C. Stay at home dad
D. Co-owner of Weasley's Wizard Wheezes

4. Who is the Headmaster/mistress of Hogwarts in *Cursed Child*?
A. Minerva McGonagall
B. Neville Longbottom
C. Hannah Abbott
D. Filius Flitwick

5. What are the names of all the second-generation children of parents who were in Harry's year at Hogwarts featured in the stage production of *Cursed Child*?
A. ______________
B. ______________
C. ______________
D. ______________
E. ______________

Jamie Parker as Harry Potter, Noma Dumezweni as Hermione Granger and Paul Thornley as Ron Weasley in costume for *Harry Potter and the Cursed Child*.

Match the Wand Movement

Can you match the spell to its wand movement as seen in the Wizarding World of Harry Potter theme parks and the *Harry Potter* mobile games?

1. *Accio*
2. *Fumos*
3. Switching Spell
4. *Aparecium*
5. *Alohomora*
6. *Mimble Wimble*
7. *Impedimenta*

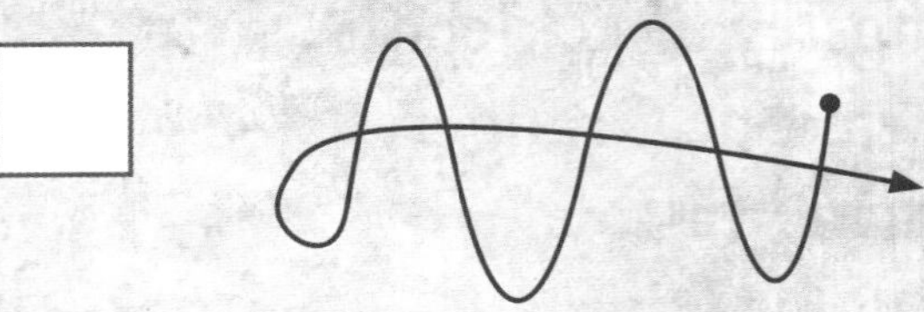

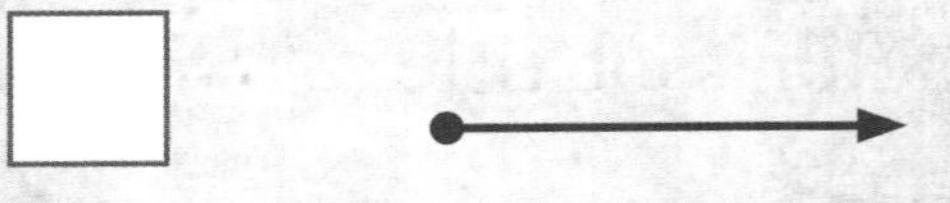

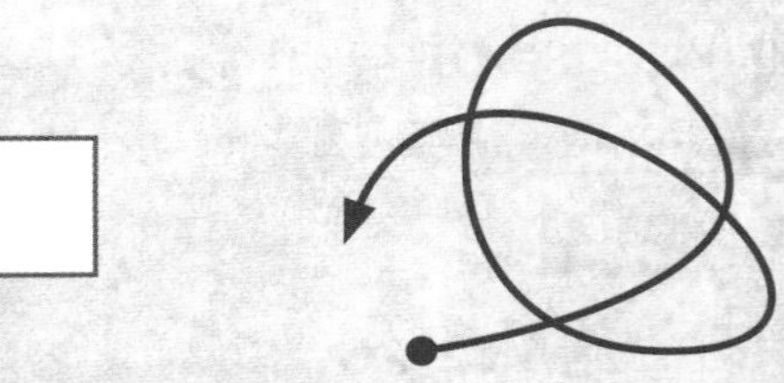

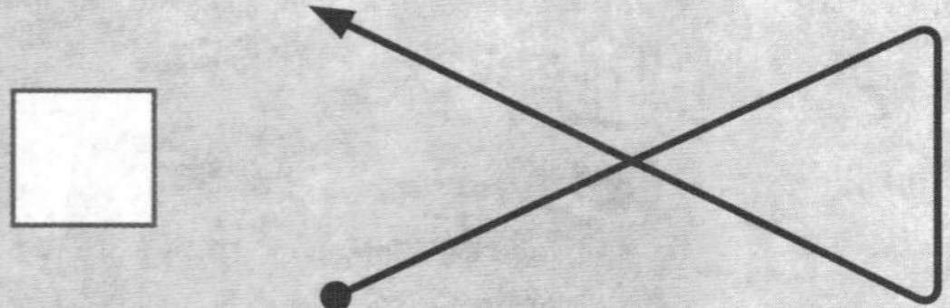

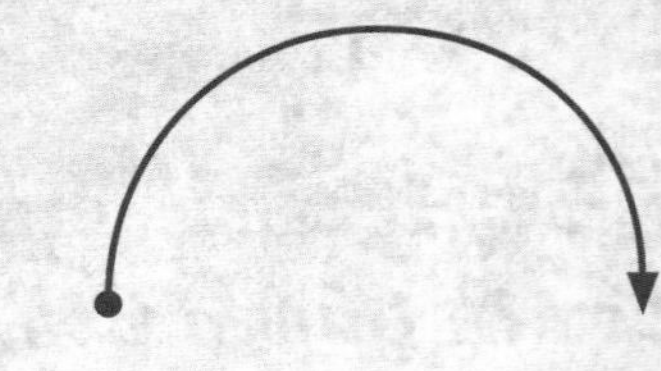

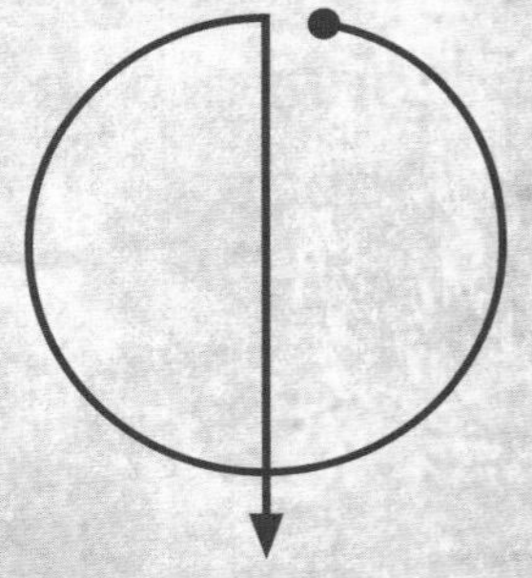

Maggie Smith as Minerva McGonagall in *Harry Potter and the Deathly Hallows: Part 2* (2011).

YEAR 1

FILL-IN-THE BLANKS: PG. 6

Hogwarts
Witchcraft
Wizardry
Voldemort
Boy
Lived
Privet Drive
Rubeus
Weasley
Hermione
Albus Dumbledore
Voldemort
Quidditch
McGonagall
Gryffindor
Three-Headed Dog
Fluffy
Music
Who Must Not Be Named
Quirrell

FIND YOUR WIZARDING WARES PGS. 8-9

1. The Leaky Cauldron
2. Florean Fortescue's Ice Cream Parlor
3. Ollivanders
4. Quality Quidditch Supplies
5. Flourish and Blotts
6. Madam Malkin's Robes for All Occasions
7. Eeylops Owl Emporium
8. Gringotts

A ROBBERY AT GRINGOTTS PG. 11

12,750 Galleons—Antique Foe-Glass
16,840 Galleons—Jeweled Pensieve
8,050 Galleons—Original Pressing, Merlin Chocolate Frog Card
14,360 Galleons—Solid Gold Omniocular
20,000 Galleons—Uncut Sapphires, Rubies and Opals

HOGWARTS CLASS OF '98 PGS. 12-13

Gryffindor:
Harry Potter
Ron Weasley
Neville Longbottom
Dean Thomas
Seamus Finnigan
Hermione Granger
Lavender Brown
Parvati Patil

Ravenclaw:
Anthony Goldstein
Michael Corner
Terry Boot
Padma Patil
Mandy Brocklehurst
Lisa Turpin

Hufflepuff:
Ernie Macmillan
Justin Finch-Fletchley
Wayne Hopkins
Hannah Abbott
Susan Bones

Slytherin:
Draco Malfoy
Vincent Crabbe
Gregory Goyle
Theodore Nott
Blaise Zabini
Pansy Parkinson
Daphne Greengrass
Millicent Bulstrode

M	G	Y	E	U	P	S	R	H	B	M	L	T	R	O	L	L
Y	Q	A	C	F	Q	X	Y	E	C	J	V	D	J	P	D	O
D	A	W	H	P	E	D	B	W	B	M	Y	B	L	A	J	R
Q	K	H	F	N	O	B	L	J	W	E	M	Z	C	U	Z	A
W	C	Z	M	U	D	D	J	R	U	D	I	H	M	F	O	Y
W	R	L	V	Y	U	W	I	S	A	E	B	I	F	H	P	A
T	I	J	T	L	C	L	L	K	V	X	W	G	X	Q	G	U
G	S	N	L	P	D	F	O	Z	C	E	N	T	A	U	R	U
L	Y	B	G	V	J	B	L	Y	A	Q	P	G	F	V	S	K
O	M	O	T	A	R	N	X	N	O	B	O	G	G	A	A	C
C	S	J	D	K	R	H	W	S	I	L	C	S	K	H	C	S
O	B	H	M	R	J	D	X	J	W	U	U	D	P	U	E	M
M	H	G	P	J	W	K	I	Z	X	Y	L	D	Q	Y	Z	R
O	E	A	M	Z	O	Q	K	U	P	B	U	C	Q	I	A	T
T	Y	R	N	B	L	X	I	Z	M	Q	S	B	A	H	H	J
O	X	L	F	O	F	V	S	I	Y	L	R	K	G	Y	H	I
R	Q	I	B	A	S	I	G	I	F	B	E	L	W	S	M	S
M	Y	C	E	R	B	D	E	Q	H	U	P	V	F	A	L	C
O	F	H	Z	H	A	A	L	N	W	W	A	W	I	F	I	A
R	I	H	O	O	N	A	H	B	B	J	R	U	V	O	U	M
T	J	D	A	U	E	S	H	J	A	A	O	X	U	R	S	D
I	Z	K	R	N	Z	R	P	A	Q	I	H	D	Q	T	N	A
S	W	N	L	D	A	Y	B	E	P	R	K	G	M	R	J	N

FIRST-YEAR CURRICULUM PGS. 14-15

Troll
Oculus Reparo
Locomotor Mortis
Wingardium Leviosa
Bezoar
Wolfsbane
Centaur
Boarhound
Garlic

HOGWARTS CURRICULUM: YEAR 1 PGS. 16-18

1. C
2. I show not your face, but your heart's desire
3. A
4. D
5. Tom Riddle
6. Peeves
7. Corned beef
8. Privet Drive
9. Halloween
10. A Pumpkin Pasty
11. A. The Dursleys
B. Mrs. Weasley
C. Hermione
D. Hagrid
E. Dumbledore (anonymously)
12. Dudley
13. Pig
14. *Wingardium Leviosa*
15. *Alohomora*
16. *Petrificus Totalus*

CHAPTER MATCHING: PG. 19

1. B 2. D 3. A 4. F 5. C 6. E

THE HOGWARTS "ALMA MATER": PG. 20

Hoggy warty; teach; bald; scabby; heads; interesting; air; flies; knowing; rot

BE THE SORTING HAT: PGS. 22-23

1. Hufflepuff
2. Ravenclaw
3. Slytherin
4. Gryffindor

NOTE: *Sometimes the Sorting Hat has a hard time choosing which House a student should be sorted into. These students are called "Hatstalls." If you sorted a character differently than the hat, perhaps they're complex!*

THE FORBIDDEN FOREST PG. 25

WANDLORE WISDOM: PG. 26

1. Harry 2. Draco 3. Ron (#1) 4. Voldemort 5. Bellatrix Lestrange 6. Hermione 7. Ron (#2) 8. Umbridge

MAGIC SHADOWS: HARRY PG. 29

TEACHER OF THE YEAR: PART 1 PG. 30

1. The Leaky Cauldron 2. Garlic 3. D 4. C 5. Oliver Wood

CHECKMATE CHALLENGE PGS. 33-35

1. Rd8# 2. Qxf7# 3. Nd4 f5# 4. Qh7# 5. Qd8# 6. Nxc4#

MUGGLENET'S EXPERT TRIVIA: PG. 36

Hankerton Humble; Minerva McGonagall; Herbert Beery; Silver Arrow

YEAR 2

FILL-IN-THE-BLANKS: PG. 40

Mirror
Erised
Sorcerer's Stone
Dobby
Ron
Fred
George
Father
Anglia
Whomping Willow
Heir
Slytherin
Chamber
Secrets
Basilisk
Hagrid
Azkaban
Ghost
Moaning Myrtle
Diary
Voldemort
Fawkes
Phoenix

NEW FRIENDS, NEW FOES PGS. 42-43

1. Aragog
2. Arthur Weasley
3. Colin Creevey
4. Dobby
5. Tom Riddle
6. Lucius Malfoy
7. Mr. Borgin
8. Moaning Myrtle
9. Gilderoy Lockhart

ARTHUR WEASLEY'S SILLY CIRCUITS: PGS. 44-45

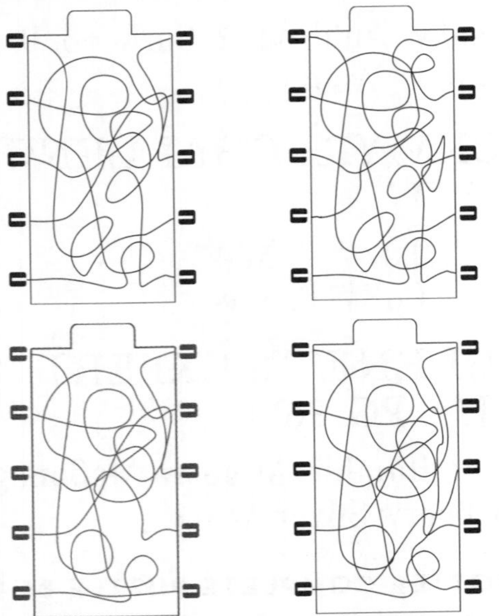

ARTHUR WEASLEY'S SILLY CIRCUITS: PGS. 46-49

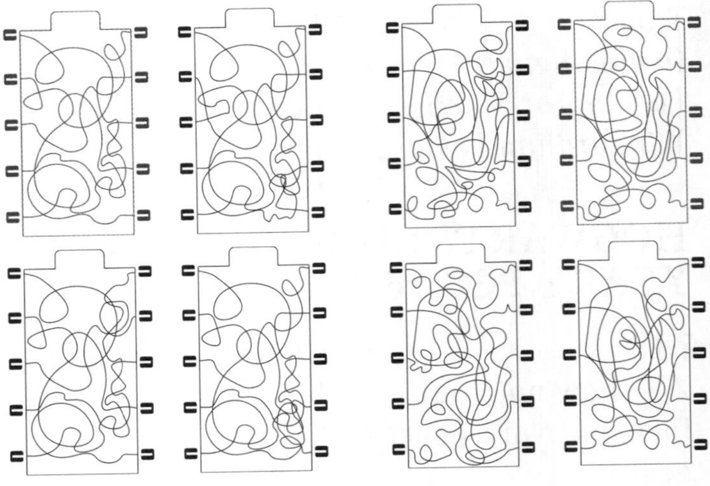

MAGIC SHADOWS: HERMIONE PG. 51

HOGWARTS CURRICULUM: YEAR 2 PGS. 52-56

1. A 2. B 3. Vladimir Putin 4. D
5. Slytherin's locket 6. B
7. C 8: Lacewing flies, leeches, powdered Bicorn horn, knotgrass, fluxweed, shredded Boomslang skin and a bit of the person you want to turn into 9. *Expelliarmus* or Disarming Charm 10. *Immobilus*
11. *Rictusempra* 12. *Serpensortia*
13. *Aparecium* 14. *Vipera Evanesca*
16. *Arania Exumai* 16. *Finite Incantatem*
17. pickled toad; hair; mine; Dark Lord
18. A, D, F, H

ARE YOU A QUIDDITCH EXPERT?: PGS. 58-59

1. Real
2. Fake
3. Real
4. Real
5. Fake
6. Real
7. Real
8. Fake

Bonus: 700

MATCH DAY LOGIC PG. 61

George Weasley	Alicia Spinnet	Adrian Pucey	Draco Malfoy
Marcus Flint	Quaffle	Katie Bell	Bludger #2
Snitch	Angelina Johnson	Bludger #1	Fred Weasley

ENEMIES OF THE HEIR BEWARE: PG. 63

1. C 2. B 3. E 4. D 5. A 6. A

TEACHER OF THE YEAR: PART 2 PG. 64

1. B 2. 10 3. D 4. A 5. Ravenclaw
6. C 7. B 8. C 9. B

GILDEROY IN PRINT: PG. 67

A, C, G, I, L, N

THE RIGHT STUFF: PGS. 68-69

Option 1

MUGGLENET'S EXPERT TRIVIA: PG. 70

Gilderoy Lockhart; XXX; 437; 199

WEASLEYS' WIZARDING CLOCK PGS. 72-73

1. Mr. Weasley 2. Percy 3. Ginny 4. Bill
5. Charlie 6. Molly Weasley 7. Fred
8. Ron 9. George

YEAR 3

FILL-IN-THE-BLANKS: PG. 76

Aunt Marge
Privet Drive
Knight Bus
Sirius Black
Azkaban
Parents
Remus Lupin
Marauder's Map
Fred
George
Peter Pettigrew
Scabbers
Sirius

ESCAPE FROM AZKABAN PG. 79

HOGWARTS CURRICULUM: YEAR 3 PGS. 80-84

1. B 2. A 3. C 4. C 5. C 6. A 7: *A Brief History of Time* by Stephen Hawking; 8. *Lumos*
9. *Riddikulus*, Laughter 10. *Bombarda*
11. C 12. C 13. *Impervius* 14. A 15. Cheering
16. *Arresto Momentum*

YEAR 3 CONT.

MAGIC SHADOWS: RON PG. 87

TEACHER OF THE YEAR: PART 3 PG. 88

1. A 2. 394 3. D 4. full moon 5. B
6. unregistered animagi
7. Mischief Managed, Snape

HOGSMEADE VILLAGE PG. 90

1. Dervish and Banges
2. The Hog's Head
3. Honeydukes
4. Hogsmeade Station
5. Zonko's Joke Shop
6. The Shrieking Shack
7. The Three Broomsticks
8. Hogsmeade Post Office
9. Madam Puddifoot's Tea Shop

HAGRID'S CARE OF MAGICAL CREATURES QUIZ: PG. 92

1. C 2. A 3. *The Monster Book of Monsters*
4. B 5. Lettuce

CARE OF MAGICAL CREATURES PG. 95

Blast-Ended Skrewt: A creature created by Hagrid by cross-breeding fire crabs with manticores.
Hippogriff: An eagle-horse hybrid that proves essential to a *Prisoner of Azkaban* escape plan.
Flobberworm: An objectively boring, herbivorous animal Draco Malfoy claims to have been bitten by.
Salamander: Not to be confused with the magic-less animal of the same name, a fire-starting lizard.
Niffler: A creature obsessed with shiny objects that becomes a main character in the *Fantastic Beasts* films.
Thestral: A horse-like creature invisible to those who have not witnessed death.
Unicorn: A creature with magical blood and a single horn on its forehead.

MONSTER BOOK OF WORD JUMBLES: PGS. 96-97

1. NIFFLER
2. DOXY
3. KAPPA
4. NUNDU
5. DIRICAWL
6. BOGGART
7. BOWTRUCKLE
8. FWOOPER
9. DEMIGUISE
10. GRAPHORN

THE JINXED GOBSTONE PG. 98

Put three marbles on each pan—for a total of six marbles on the scale—and leave two marbles off. Compare the six marbles on the scale—if one pan is heavier than the other, you only have to focus on those three. You compare two of those three marbles to each other on the scale. If they are the same weight, the third is the heaviest. If one is heavier than the other, then that's the jinxed one. If, when comparing the six marbles, you find that both sides are equal, then you know that the heaviest marble has to be one of the two marbles that are not on the scale. This means you only have to compare those two remaining marbles and you have the heaviest marble in two measurements.

HERMIONE'S IMPOSSIBLE SCHEDULE: PG. 101

1. Potions
2. Defense Against the Dark Arts
3. Care of Magical Creatures
4. Arithmancy
5. Divination
6. Muggle Studies
7. Herbology
8. Transfiguration
9. Charms
10. Ancient Runes
11. History of Magic
12. Astronomy

THE EYE OF THE SEER: PG. 102

1. True
2. False (date is wrong)
3. False (around Easter)
4. True (Dumbledore dies 2 years later)
5. False (Parvati, not Padma)
6. True
7. True
8. True

MUGGLENET'S EXPERT TRIVIA: PG. 104

11; 6; Males have stingers, females have suckers; Dougal McGregor

MARAUDER'S MAP: PGS. 106-107

1. The Hog's Head
2. Hogsmeade
3. The Shrieking Shack
4. The Room of Requirement
5. Hogwarts

YEAR 4

FILL-IN-THE-BLANKS: PG. 110

World Cup
Irish
Bulgarian
The Dark Mark
Mad-Eye Moody
Triwizard
Hogwarts
Durmstrang
Beauxbatons
Goblet of Fire
Cedric Diggory
Viktor Krum
Fleur Delacour
Peter Pettigrew

DIAGON ALLEY MIX-UP PGS. 112-113

A3: Rotated 180°
A7: Flipped on the vertical axis
B1: Rotated 180°
B2: Flipped on the vertical axis
B7: Flipped on the horizontal axis
C6: Flipped on the vertical axis
C8: Flipped on the vertical axis
D3: Flipped on the vertical axis
F1: Rotated 180°
F2: Flipped on the horizontal axis
F3: Flipped on the vertical axis
F7: Flipped on the vertical axis

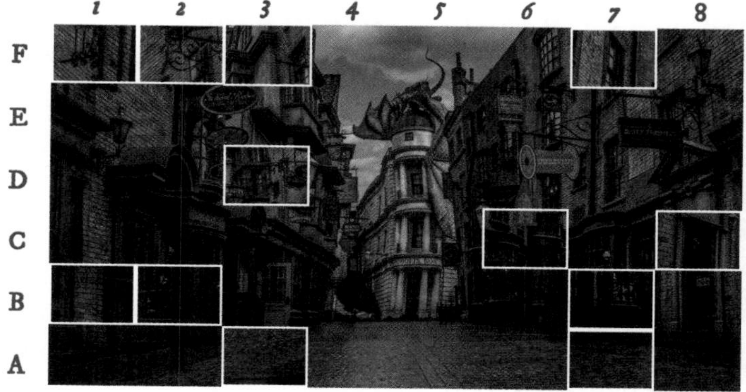

THE QUIDDITCH WORLD CUP PG. 114

1. A 2. B 3. C 4. B 5. B 6. C
7. Wronski Feint 8. Cover their ears
9. 170, 160

THE CHAMPIONSHIP TEAMS PG. 117

Ireland:
McGillicuddy, O'Hara, O'Brian

Bulgaria:
Zhukov, Kornova, Nabokov

YEAR 4 CONT.

PROFESSIONAL TEAMS OF BRITAIN AND IRELAND PG. 118

1. Ballycastle Bats
2. Puddlemere United
3. Montrose Magpies
4. Kenmare Kestrels
5. Tutshill Tornados
6. Pride of Portree
7. Appleby Arrows
8. Caerphilly Catapults
9. Holyhead Harpies
10. Wimbourne Wasps
11. Chudley Cannons
12. Wigtown Wanderers
13. Falmouth Falcons

HOGWARTS CURRICULUM: YEAR 4 PGS. 120-124

1. A 2. B 3. C 4. C 5. A 6: 42 hours 7. *Accio*
8. Banishing Charm 9. *Sonorous*
10. *Morsmordre* 11. *Stupefy* 12. *Reductor*
13. Bubble-Head Charm 14. *Impedimenta*
15. Four-Point

THE WORLD OF WIZARDING SCHOOLS PG. 127

1. Castelobruxo
2. Uagadou
3. Mahoutokoro
4. Ilvermorny
5. Hogwarts
6. Durmstrang
7. Beauxbatons

THE YULE BALL: PG. 128

Harry Potter - Parvati Patil
Ron Weasley - Padma Patil
Hermione Granger - Viktor Krum
Cedric Diggory - Cho Chang
Ginny Weasley - Neville Longbottom
Fleur Delacour - Roger Davies
Seamus Finnigan - Lavender Brown
Fred Weasley - Angelina Johnson

TEACHER OF THE YEAR: PART 4 PG. 130

1. Rosier 2. B 3. C 4. B 5. Auror
6. B 7. Trunk, Imperius

THE TRIWIZARD TOURNAMENT: PG. 132

The First Task:
1. C 2. rock, dog 3. C

The Second Task:
1. B 2. 45, Cedric Diggory
3. Ron Weasley, Gabrielle Delacour

The Third Task:
1. C 2. spider 3. Portkey

THE TRIWIZARD MAZE: PG. 134

VOLDEMORT RETURNS: PG. 136

1. C 2. C 3. Unicorn, snake, Nagini
4. Imperius Curse, bow 5. B 6. C
7. *Expelliarmus* 8. A

MUGGLENET'S EXPERT TRIVIA: PG. 138

Trans-species transformation; Remus Lupin; Hippocampus; Basilisk

YEAR 5

FILL-IN-THE-BLANKS: PG. 142

Albus Dumbledore
Cornelius Fudge
Order of the Phoenix
Death Eaters
Sirius Black
Nymphadora Tonks
12 Grimmauld Place
Occlumency
Snape
Ministry of Magic or Department of Mysteries
Prophecy
Sirius

LOST IN MUGGLE LONDON PGS. 144-145

Covent Garden

YOUR O.W.L. EXAMS: PGS. 146-152

1. B 2. C 3. A 4. A 5. D 6. C 7. B 8. C 9. B
10. Draught of Peace, Properties of Moonstone, Varieties of Venom Antidotes, Strengthening Solution 11. A 12. B
13. Stag, Jack Russell Terrier, Otter, Horse, Swan, Hare, Fox, Boar 14. Avada Kedavra, Imperio, Crucio 15. D 16. A 17. C 18. B
19. live, survives 20. D 21. A 22. B

YOUR O.W.L. EXAMS: PG. 152

23.

A. Harry saves Dudley and himself from dementors.
B. Members of the Order of the Phoenix rescue Harry from the Dursleys and take him to Sirius's childhood home.
C. Harry has his hearing at the Ministry of Magic for using magic outside of Hogwarts.
D. Harry discovers what has been pulling the seemingly horseless carriages at Hogwarts.
E. Harry receives his first detention from Umbridge and learns the cost of telling "lies."
F. Umbridge is appointed High Inquisitor.
G. Dumbledore's Army holds its first meeting.
H. Mr.Weasley is attacked by Voldemort's snake while on Order of the Phoenix duty.
I. Azkaban experiences a mass breakout, which includes the escape of Bellatrix Lestrange.
J. Hagrid shows Harry and Hermione what he's been hiding in the Forbidden Forest.
K. Harry, Ron, Hermione, Ginny, Neville and Luna travel to the Department of Mysteries after Harry has a vision of Sirius being tortured by Voldemort there.
L. Padfoot has his last laugh

THE HEADS OF HOGWARTS PGS. 154-155

1. Dilys Derwent
2. Dexter Fortescue
3. Eupraxia Mole
4. Everard
5. Phineas Nigellus Black
6. Armando Dippet
7. Dolores Umbridge
8. Albus Dumbledore
9. Severus Snape
10. Minerva McGonagall

YEAR 5 CONT.

THE EXPLODING SNAP TEST PGS. 156-159

3 of Clubs: Each row's two black cards add up to the value of its one red card. Each row has a red card, a club and a spade.

4 of hearts: Each row's first entry is doubled to get the second entry, which is doubled to get the third. Each row has one black card, one heart and one diamond.

8 of spades: Each row consists of cards of a single color, alternating suits by card. Each row's first card has two subtracted from it to get the second, which has four added to it to get the third.

TEACHER OF THE YEAR: PART 5 PG. 160

1. A 2. B 3. Slytherin 4. Draco Malfoy, Vincent Crabbe, Gregory Goyle, Pansy Parkinson, Millicent Bullstrode, Graham Montague, Cassius Warrington 5. C

DECREES OF SEPARATION PGS. 162-163

Real Decrees: 1, 4, 5, 7, 9

MIDNIGHT INVESTIGATION PGS. 164-165

Professor Umbridge

THE MINISTRY OF MAGIC PG. 166

MUGGLENET'S EXPERT TRIVIA: PG. 168

Silvanus Kettleburn; Apollyon Pringle; Ferrets; 16

YEAR 6

FILL-IN-THE-BLANKS: PG. 172

Albus Dumbledore
Voldemort
Wizarding War
Death Eaters
Slughorn
Snape
Half-Blood Prince
Horcruxes
Ginny
Draco Malfoy
Albus Dumbledore
Snape

THE LOCATION CODE PGS. 174-175

1. The Burrow
2. Little Hangleton
3. Grimmauld Place
4. Spinner's End
5. Madam Malkin
6. Ollivanders
7. Zonko's
8. Twilfitt and Tatting's

HOGWARTS CURRICULUM: YEAR 6 PGS. 176-180

1. B 2. A 3. C 4. A 5. A 6. C 7. C
8. Rembrandt 9. *Sectumsempra*
10. *Muffliato* 11. *Aguamenti* 12. Argus Filch
13. *Vulnera Sanentur*
14. 1. C 2. E 3. B 4. G 5. F 6. A 7. D

PENSIEVE LESSONS: PG. 183

1. Little Hangleton 2. Revulsion
3. Parseltongue 4. Hermione
5. You'll go wrong, boy, mark my words
6. Hepzibah Smith

THE HORCRUX CHRONICLES PGS. 184-185

1. Hogwarts; Diary; Ginny Weasley
2. Ring; Marvolo Gaunt; Deathly Hallow
3. Cup; Hufflepuff; Salazar Slytherin
4. Ravenclaw; the Grey Lady; Diadem
5. Living; Nagini; Bertha Jorkins; Harry Potter

CODED COMMON ROOM PASSWORDS: PGS. 188-189

1. CAPUT DRACONIS
2. MIMBULUS MIMBLETONIA
3. FORTUNA MAJOR
4. FAIRY LIGHTS
5. ODDSBODIKINS
6. BALDERDASH

THE LIONS OF GRYFFINDOR PG. 191

1. Angelina Johnson
2. Andrew Kirke
3. Alicia Spinnet
4. Cormac McLaggen
5. Demelza Robins
6. Dean Thomas
7. Fred Weasley
8. George Weasley
9. Ginny Weasley
10. Jimmy Peakes
11. Jack Sloper
12. Katie Bell
13. Oliver Wood
14. Ron Weasley
15. Ritchie Coote

MUGGLENET'S EXPERT TRIVIA: PG. 192

28; Toasting her students with a two-handled cup; Wilhelmina; Crumpets

THE NOBLE AND MOST ANCIENT HOUSE OF BLACK PG. 195

1. Phineas Nigellus
2. Cygnus Black
3. Irma Crabbe
4. Walburga Black
5. Sirius Black
6. Regulus Black
7. Andromeda Black
8. Narcissa Black

THE HALF-BLOOD PRINCE'S TEXTBOOK: PGS. 196-197

1. A 2. C 3. D 4. D 5. B 6. C 7. C 8. C 9. D 10. A

YEAR 7

FILL-IN-THE-BLANKS: PG. 200

Hogwarts
Horcruxes
Bill Weasley
Fleur Delacour
Ministry of Magic
Ron
Locket
Slytherin
Dumbledore's Army
Snape
Neville Longbottom
Nagini

THE SEVEN POTTERS: PG. 203

1. Hermione Granger 2. Fred Weasley 3. Fleur Delacour 4. Mundungus Fletcher 5. Harry Potter 6. Ron Weasley 7. George Weasley

DUMBLEDORE'S WILL: PG. 205

1. Percival, Wulfric, Brian 2. Bilius, Deluminator, Remember me 3. Jean, copy, *The Tales of Beedle the Bard*, entertaining, informative 4. James, snitch, caught, Quidditch match, perseverance, skill

YEAR 7 CONT.

N.E.W.T. EXAMS: PGS. 206-212

1. Food 2. Metamorphosis 3. Into nonbeing 4. Greece 5. *Protego* 6. Undetectable extension charm 7. Slughorn 8. *Arresto Momentum* 9. The Hog's Head 10. *Confringo* 11. *Defodio* 12. Dittany 13. Felix Felicis 14. Everlasting elixirs 15. Libatius Borage 16. *Salvio Hexia* 17. Tongue-tying curse 18. *Expelliarmus* 19. Peter Pettigrew 20. 200,000

ESCAPE FROM MALFOY MANOR PG. 215

THE TALE OF THE THREE BROTHERS: PG. 217

1. *Beedle the Bard* 2. midnight, twilight, 3. bridge, river 4. powerful wand, win 5. Resurrection 6. elude, Cloak of Invisibility 7. eight 8. three, veil 9. greeted, old friend, his son

A TRUE GRYFFINDOR PGS. 218-219

THE UNITED KINGDOM OF MAGIC: PGS. 220-221

1. Platform 9¾
2. Diagon Alley
3. Hogsmeade
4. Hogwarts
5. The Forest of Dean
6. Cokeworth
7. 10 Downing Street
8. Little Whinging, Surrey
9. Godric's Hollow
10. Ottery St. Catchpole

MUGGLENET'S EXPERT TRIVIA: PG. 222

Chimeras; A fire-breathing chicken; 328; 11

WORLDWIDE WIZARDING PGS. 224-225

1. *Fantastic Beasts and Where to Find Them*, France, French; 2. *Harry Potter and the Order of the Phoenix*, Finland, Finnish; 3. *The Tales of Beedle the Bard*, Japan, Japanese; 4. *Harry Potter and the Half-Blood Prince*, The Netherlands, Dutch; 5. *Harry Potter and the Deathly Hallows*, China, Mandarin; 6. *Harry Potter and the Goblet of Fire*, Italy, Italian; 7. *Harry Potter and the Chamber of Secrets*, Germany, German; 8. *Harry Potter and the Sorcerer's Stone*, Ireland, Irish Gaelic; 9. *Harry Potter and the Prisoner of Azkaban*, South Korea, Korean

CURSED CATCH-UP: PG. 227

1. A 2. B 3. D 4. A 5. A. James Sirius Potter B. Albus Severus Potter C. Lily Luna Potter D. Rose Granger-Weasley E. Scorpius Malfoy

MATCH THE WAND MOVEMENT: PG. 228

3. Switching Spell
2. *Fumos*
4. *Aparecium*
7. *Impedimenta*
6. *Mimble Wimble*
1. *Accio*
5. *Alohomora*